A Practical Guide to Privacy in Libraries

A Practical Guide
to Privacy in Libraries

Paul Pedley

 facet
publishing

© Paul Pedley 2020

Published by Facet Publishing,
7 Ridgmount Street, London WC1E 7AE
www.facetpublishing.co.uk

Facet Publishing is wholly owned by CILIP: the Library and Information Association.

The author asserts his moral right to be identified as such in accordance with the terms of the Copyright, Designs and Patents Act 1988.

Except as otherwise permitted under the Copyright, Designs and Patents Act 1988 this publication may only be reproduced, stored or transmitted in any form or by any means, with the prior permission of the publisher, or, in the case of reprographic reproduction, in accordance with the terms of a licence issued by The Copyright Licensing Agency. Enquiries concerning reproduction outside those terms should be sent to Facet Publishing, 7 Ridgmount Street, London WC1E 7AE.

Every effort has been made to contact the holders of copyright material reproduced in this text, and thanks are due to them for permission to reproduce the material indicated. If there are any queries please contact the publisher.

British Library Cataloguing in Publication Data
A catalogue record for this book is available from the British Library.

ISBN 978-1-78330-468-4 (paperback)
ISBN 978-1-78330-469-1 (hardback)

First published 2020

Text printed on FSC accredited material.

Typeset in 10/13 pt University Old Style and Humanist 521 by Flagholme Publishing Services.
Printed and made in Great Britain by CPI Group (UK) Ltd, Croydon, CR0 4YY.

Contents

Disclaimer

Paul Pedley is not a lawyer and is unable to give legal advice. The contents of this book do not constitute legal advice and should not be relied upon in that way.

List of tables, figures and checklists

Tables

Figures

Checklists

List of abbreviations

AIIM	Association for Information and Image Management
ALA	American Library Association
API	Application programming interface
ARL	Association of Research Libraries
BDSG	Bundesdatenschutzgesetz (Federal Data Protection Act)
BIC	Book Industry Communication
BYOD	Bring your own device
CASSIE	Computer Access Software Solution
CCTV	Closed circuit television
CHIS	Covert human intelligence sources
CIA	The CIA triad of Confidentiality, Integrity and Availability
CILIP	CILIP: the Library and Information Association
CIPFA	Chartered Institute of Public Finance and Accountancy
CRB	Criminal Records Bureau
DBS	Disclosure and Barring Service
DDOS	Distributed denial of service attack
DOB	Date of birth
DPA	Data Protection Act 2018
DPC	Data Protection Commissioner (Ireland)
DPIA	Data protection impact assessment
ECHR	European Convention on Human Rights
ECJ	European Court of Justice (also known as CJEU)
EEA	European Economic Area
FAIFE	Freedom of Access to Information and Freedom of Expression (FAIFE) (an advisory committee of IFLA)
FCI	Framework of contextual integrity
FOI	Freedom of information
GA	Google Analytics
GDPR	General Data Protection Regulation
HaaS	Hardware as a service
ICO	Information Commissioner's Office
IDS	Intrusion detection system
IFLA	International Federation of Library Associations
IFLA FAIFE	Freedom of Access to Information and Freedom of Expression - an advisory committee of IFLA
IMSI	International mobile subscriber identity

LACA	(UK) Libraries and Archives Copyright Alliance
LFI	Library Freedom Institute
LGBT	Lesbian, gay, bisexual, transgender
LGMA	Local Government Management Agency
LMS	Library management system
LWW	Library Without Walls
MAIPLE	Managing Access to the Internet in Public Libraries
NISO	National Information Standards Organization
NSA	(US) National Security Agency
OIF	Office for Intellectual Freedom (of the American Library Association)
OPLIS	Online privacy literacy scale
PECR	Privacy and Electronic Communications (EC Directive) Regulations 2003 as amended
PIA	Privacy Impact Assessment (see also DPIA)
PII	Personally identifiable information
PRISM	Code name for an NSA surveillance programme
RFID	Radio frequency identification
RIPA	Regulation of Investigatory Powers Act 2000
RTBF	Right To Be Forgotten
SaaS	Software as a Service
SALS	Southern Adirondack Library System
SDI	Selective dissemination of information
SIP2	Standard interchange protocol
SQL	Structured query language
TLS	Transport layer security
TOS	Terms of service
TOSDR	Terms of service didn't read
URL	Uniform resource locator
USP	Unique selling point
VLE	Virtual learning environment
WHELF	Wales Higher Education Libraries Forum

Table of legislation

List of cases

CHAPTER 1

Setting the scene

Defining privacy is complex. It can be 'a claim, a right, an interest, a value, a preference, or merely a state of existence' (Nissenbaum, 2010, 2). Given that privacy is such a complex issue, it is hardly surprising to find that it is by no means easy to document the diverse range of ways in which privacy issues impact upon the delivery of library services. This book tries, nevertheless, to do precisely that.

The book aims to be as practical as possible. The intention is to help library staff become more privacy-conscious, to have confidentiality and privacy considerations in their minds when they go about delivering the services that they offer. Throughout the text there are numerous pointers to the practical ways in which library and information professionals can further develop and enhance their approach to privacy.

The book tries to do this by:

- covering a wide range of practical examples of the privacy issues that can arise in a library context (Chapter 3)
- setting out a number of in-depth library privacy case studies (Chapter 4)
- giving examples of data breaches which have taken place within a library setting, and the lessons we can learn from them (Chapter 6)
- acknowledging that their reliance on commercial products from external vendors in order to be able to provide their services requires them to work with those vendors to achieve the best possible user privacy protections (Chapter 11).

The book also covers a range of tools through which libraries are able to communicate how they handle the personal data of their users, whilst also ensuring that they are following best practice:

- privacy policy statements (Chapter 8)
- privacy audits (Chapter 9)
- data protection impact assessments (Chapter 10).

Finally, the book concludes by highlighting a series of practical steps that can be taken to protect the privacy of library users. These include steps to protect privacy on public access terminals; education and training initiatives; information security measures; and vendor management (Chapter 12). It is necessary first, though, to set the scene:

- How did library privacy issues arise in the past?
- How have the privacy risks changed?
- Why does it matter?

Once those questions have been considered, the book then moves on to outline the ways in which privacy is regulated in the UK (Chapter 2), before moving on to look at a wide range of examples of the ways in which privacy considerations arise in a library context (Chapter 3).

1.1   Examples of how privacy issues arose in the 19th and 20th centuries

1.1.1   Browne issue system

For much of the 20th century library loans were recorded using the Browne issue system, a system devised by Nina Browne in 1895. When a user borrowed a book the librarian took one of the reader's borrowing cards (these were often in the form of a folded piece of card which acted as a pocket within which a card from a book could be filed), removed the book's own card and then filed the two together. These were typically filed in wooden trays with the cards arranged in order of the date of issue. When the book was returned to the library, the librarian would find the cards by checking the most recent date appearing on the issue slip found in the front of the book. The user's borrowing card would be returned to them. Meanwhile the book's card would be placed back into the book itself ready for it to be reshelved.

The Browne issue system was very respectful of privacy. However, the system did pose several threats to the security of library users' personal data when compared to the potential risks posed by the computerised systems currently used for managing library loans:

- Paper records are considered to be a higher risk to the security of data than electronic records because there is no backup. Once a file is lost, all the information is gone. Data loss is a key risk in information security.
- Paper files can be more easily stolen or misplaced.

But the Browne system can also be said to have posed few threats to the privacy of library users' data:

- The link between the borrower and the item borrowed was broken as soon as the book was returned to the library.
- Borrowing records were kept in date order rather than order of borrower. To see a full list of what a borrower had on loan at any one time would have required a manual check through the entire set of cards, as the user may have borrowed books on several different dates. Even then it would only have told you what someone currently had out on loan, rather than their complete borrowing history.
- As the records were paper-based it was impossible to analyse the loans - for example, trying to find out which users currently had books out on loan by a particular author, on a particular subject or by a particular publisher.
- There was no backup of the loan records.
- The records could only be accessed on library premises and were only accessed by relevant staff, not remotely from another location.

The demise of the Browne issue system largely occurred from the 1970s onwards as a result of technological advances such as the use of barcodes and scanners and the emergence of computerised library systems.

1.1.2   Cards used to sign out a book

Instead of using the Browne issue system some libraries relied instead on the use of a single card to record both the item borrowed and the borrower's details. This alternative to the Browne issue system didn't have one of the key privacy benefits that the Browne system offered. Using a single card for each book means that the card was, in effect, building up a list of everyone who had borrowed that particular book. Even after the book had been returned to the library, the link between borrower and the title borrowed remained.

At the top of each card would be the classification mark, the title and author of the book. Then underneath this the main part of the card would have two columns. One would show the borrower's signature, the other column would show the date on which the book had been borrowed.

Anyone browsing the shelves would be able to look at the ticket in the front of the book and they would see a list of everyone who has ever borrowed that particular book. This is a breach of library user privacy. The book could potentially be on a difficult or embarrassing topic. Knowing the names of everyone who has read a book on pregnancy or abortion or bulimia is highly sensitive and likely to be embarrassing. There is also a real danger that one of the special categories of personal data (also known as sensitive personal data - see Figure 1.1 on the next page) will be processed. The types of data that fall into this category are listed in GDPR Article 9. It might, for example, point towards someone's political views, their religious views, their sexuality, or to the current state of their health.

Personal data revealing . . .
- racial or ethnic origin
- political opinions
- religious or philosophical beliefs
- trade union membership
- genetic data
- biometric data for the purpose of uniquely identifying a natural person
- health data
- data concerning a natural person's sex life or sexual orientation.

Figure 1.1 *Sensitive personal data*

The saving grace of the single card system to record loans data was that precisely because the data was held in analogue form, the extent of any privacy breach was extremely limited.

1.1.3   Library Awareness Program

The Library Awareness Program is the name of a counterintelligence activity undertaken by the Federal Bureau of Investigation (FBI) in the 1980s. Foerstel (1991) documents attempts by the FBI to involve library staff members in its pursuit of Soviets who, the FBI claimed, were recruiting agents and gathering scientific and military intelligence in public, academic and special libraries. Foerstel said that

> . . . the FBI's Library Awareness Program, the Bureau's most extended and notorious attempt at library surveillance, must be considered in the context of the many recent federal attempts to restrict information access, but the uniqueness of this program is its attempt to recruit librarians as counterintelligence 'assets' to monitor suspicious library users and report their reading habits to the FBI.
>
> (Foerstel, 1991, 2)

1.1.4   Publishing lists of borrowers with overdue books

In 1987 the Lebanon (IN) Public Library in the USA published a list of borrowers with overdue books in the local newspaper and matched their names against titles *like Two Guys Noticed Me . . . and Other Miracles, What About Teenage Marriage?, What Only a Mother Can Tell You About Having a Baby, The Myth of Senility'* and *I Should Have Seen it Coming When the Rabbit Died.* According to Wiegand (2002), it was reported at the time that ALA's Office for Intellectual Freedom (OIF) indicated that patron confidentiality did not apply when users fail to return a book. Publishing the list of names 'does what they [the library] want it to', an OIF staff member said at the time, adding that the action 'brings the books back'.

1.1.5 Names of people requesting German-language books turned over to the authorities

In November 1917, during World War I, the San Francisco Public Library removed all German-language books from its shelves, thereby forcing patrons to come to the circulation desk to request them. The names of people who requested German-language books at the public libraries in San Francisco, St Louis, District of Columbia, Salt Lake City, Los Angeles and Philadelphia were regularly turned over to the authorities for investigation (Wiegand, 2002).

1.1.6 Library patron numbers used for several purposes

In 2007 a librarian mentioned how library patron numbers were the same as student lunch numbers. The practice of using the patron's library number for several purposes increases the risk of that number being learned by others. Once armed with that information they could see what books a user had borrowed by entering their library number (Adams, 2008).

Nowadays, public libraries issue library users with library cards along with PIN numbers. The above scenario would not be possible where users are required to enter a combination of both their library card number and their PIN number to log into the library management system and access their borrowing record. Simply knowing someone's library number would not be sufficient.

1.1.7 Russian revolutionary emigrés' use of the British Museum Library

In the 19th century the British Museum Library was used by numbers of Russian revolutionary emigrés, including Herzen, Lenin, Kropotkin, Kravchinskii and others. The lists of library ticket holders still survive, but one thing that they reveal is the frequent use of pseudonyms by the emigrés so as to avoid the attentions of the Okhrana, the Russian secret service. Leo von Beitner, a British Museum reader, was later exposed as an informer and at one point the emigrés suspected that a library staff member was supplying the Okhrana with their addresses (Henderson, 1991, cited in Sturges, Iliffe and Dearnley, 2001).

1.2 Why are the risks to library user privacy so much bigger in the 21st century than before?

The risks to library user privacy are exponentially greater in the 21st century than they were in the preceding century for a number of reasons:

- computer systems create records where none existed before
- library services go beyond library walls
- the library network is part of a larger networked world

- advances in the analytical capabilities of the technology
- libraries are simultaneously service providers and consumers: they rely on commercial products from external vendors in order to provide their services:
  - e-book platforms
  - discovery services
  - RFID (to enable self checkout, stock control)
  - library management systems
  - content delivery platforms
- use of cloud solutions to deliver services:
  - SaaS services
  - IaaS services
  - HaaS services
- offshoring and outsourcing of library services
- data being shared with third parties:
  - vendors
  - advertisers
  - social networks
  - e-book retailers
  - search engines
  - analytics companies
  - internet service providers.

The types of technology that have had an impact on library services in recent years include:

- algorithms
- artificial intelligence
- augmented reality
- authentication methods
- big data
- blogging
- CCTV
- cloud computing
- data analytics
- data mining
- geolocation
- intelligent bookshelves (RFID)
- internet of things
- learning analytics
- mobile technology

- quantum computing
- RFID
- social networking
- Wi-Fi hotspots.

Corporate entities do not just rely on the data that has been gathered about individuals. They go further and use that for profiling purposes. Mai (2016) uses the term 'datafication' to consider a new model, the datafication model, wherein new personal information is deduced by employing predictive analytics on already gathered data.

The privacy of library users needs to be protected. This is not exclusively a question of the library looking after the personal data of its users. The delivery of library services takes place through a complex ecosystem involving library staff, volunteers, library users, library vendors, partners and a whole host of third and possibly fourth parties:

First party (consumer/individual transaction)
Second party (vendor/provider of products and services)
Third party (legal data-sharing partners)
Fourth party (illegal entities)

Figure 1.2 *The parties involved in processing personal data* (Source: Conger, Pratt and Loch's (2013) expanded privacy model)

In the past, according to Green (2016), there were two main practical limits on unauthorised data disclosures: the amount of data in one place a hacker could access; and the narrow scope of what could be done with the data once captured.

Neither of these limits still applies.

⊷ Useful resource

The Lightbeam Firefox add-in (https://addons.mozilla.org/en-GB/firefox/addon/lightbeam) tracks websites visited and makes it easy to see the third parties who have also had access to your data.

At the CILIP Privacy Briefing on 28 November 2017, McMenemy made the point that:

Our commitment to patron privacy is significantly challenged by some of our own activities:

- **Internet filtering:** direct challenge to the information seeking of our users
- **Use of 3rd parties in service delivery:** are we open about who, why, and what they will do with user data?
- **Learner analytics:** are we in effect spying on our users' activities?

(McMenemy, 2017)

The 21st-century risks to library user privacy are the result of:

- the range and volume of personal data collected
- the capacity to analyse, predict and derive findings from that data through the use of algorithms, data analytics and profiling
- the risks of a data breach occurring when library services are delivered through a complex ecosystem involving a range of stakeholders
- the potential risks posed by external entities when libraries are involved in outsourcing or offshoring, or where they use cloud computing services.

1.3   Why is the privacy of library users important?

In recent years privacy issues have risen up the agenda in terms of their importance. A white paper (Iron Mountain and Association for Information and Image Management, 2015) found that risk, security and data privacy topped the list of desired skills for organisations.

Members of the public are more aware of privacy issues for various reasons, including:

- the number and scale of data breaches
- the Edward Snowden revelations
- the Cambridge Analytica scandal
- repeated calls for the tech companies to be more strictly regulated
- extensive and wide-ranging press coverage of the changes to data protection law brought about by GDPR
- the hostile environment policies which have included deporting of homeless people using charity and NHS data.

Other important examples, though not quite so recent, include:

- the Milly Dowler phone hacking case
- the revelations relating to the surveillance of Doreen Lawrence and her husband Neville in the aftermath of Stephen Lawrence's death.

Members of the public are also more aware of their data protection rights. Those rights have been expanded as a result of the passing of the GDPR and the Data Protection Act 2018.

Protecting the privacy of library users matters. It cannot be seen in isolation, purely as a concern of the library and information profession. In order to understand the issues involved, one has to take account of the wider context. The business environment in which the big tech companies and businesses more generally operate places a high value on data. They see it as a commodity like oil or gold. They believe in gathering as much data as possible, and using this for their own ends. An article in *The Economist* from 2017 declared that 'the world's most valuable resource is no longer oil, but data', and that 'by collecting more data, a firm has more scope to improve its products, which attracts more users, generating even more data, and so on' (Economist, 2017).

A failure to protect the privacy of library users can easily lead to the following scenario:

> If you're reading on a device, your reading behaviors will be correlated with those of multitudes of other people. If someone who has a reading pattern similar to yours bought something after it was pitched in a particular way, then the odds become higher that you will get the same pitch.
>
> (Lanier, 2018, 32)

Zuboff believes that:

> . . . the operator of a search engine is liable to affect significantly the fundamental rights to privacy and to the protection of personal data. In the light of the potential seriousness of the interference it cannot be justified by merely the economic interest which the operator of such an engine has in that processing.
>
> (Zuboff, 2019, 59)

Zuboff's viewpoint is relevant to and valid for library vendors just as much as it is for the big tech companies. She talks of surveillance capitalism, which aims to predict and modify human behaviour as a means to produce revenue and market control. All of this is possible as a result of the vast quantities of data about individuals which companies and governments collect and use.

Mayer-Schönberger and Cukier (2013, 151) believe that with big data promising valuable insights to those who analyse it, all the signs seem to point to a further surge in others gathering, storing and reusing our personal data. The size and scale of data collections will increase by leaps and bounds as storage costs continue to plummet and analytical tools become ever more powerful. They make the point that the internet age threatened privacy, but that big data endangers it even more so. The change of scale brought about by big data is transformational because big data makes it possible to make predictions about people to judge and punish them even before they've acted. Doing this negates ideas of fairness, justice and free will.

Angwin (2014) revealed that it was practically impossible to opt out of pervasive surveillance by governments and companies without practically opting out of society and human contact itself.

It is in this context that one needs to consider the value the corporate world would place on the sorts of personal data that libraries are dealing with each and every day. Nearly two decades ago Johnston (2000) called library circulation systems a 'social surveillance system' because of what you can learn about someone from their library borrowing record. In the period since that assertion was made, the amount of user data routinely collected and processed by libraries has grown exponentially. It now goes far beyond a user's borrowing history, and now includes (but is not limited to):

- computer usage logs
- printing history
- web browsing history
- Wi-Fi usage logs
- library users':
  - borrowing history
  - reservation history
  - payments history
- online catalogue usage logs
- website analytics
- CCTV logs
- location data from RFID tags.

1.3.1   The chilling effect

The 'chilling effect' refers to the phenomenon whereby people either know or suspect that they are being monitored, and change their behaviour accordingly. Caldwell-Stone (2012) defines library users' information privacy as the right to read and inquire anything, without the fear of being judged or punished. You might choose not to visit certain websites if you thought that the government could use this as evidence against you.

Reading is often an act of fantasy, and fantasy cannot be made criminal without imperilling the freedom to think as one wishes (Richards, 2008, 442). The chilling effect of such an intrusion into intellectual privacy could cause people to skew their reading habits towards the bland and the boring for fear of attracting the attention of the government.

⊷ Remember

Governments can chill the rights of citizens through sloppy legislation, but professionals can also do so through sloppy practice and procedure.

Examples of the chilling effect:

- A study at Central Michigan University's Park Library found that LGBT material was borrowed 20% more if done by self-check than using the traditional circulation desk (Mathson and Hancks, 2008).
- Following the Snowden revelations of mass surveillance, users' search behaviour changed, including a drop in search traffic for terms rated as being personally sensitive according to Marthews and Tucker (2015). They found a statistically significant 5% reduction in Google searches for certain privacy-sensitive search terms after June 2013. Their study not only provides evidence of chilling effects, but also offers a research design that may be employed to study chilling effects in other online contexts.
- In Norway you can look up anybody's tax records. It was once possible to do so anonymously. However, people must now log onto the tax system and thereby leave a trail of which records they have looked at. When the change was made, the number of searches fell by 90%.
- A young woman stopped short of printing out her research on sexually transmitted diseases when she learnt that the printer was at the front desk (Fillo, 1999).

1.3.2   Nothing to hide

When people object to surveillance they are told rather tritely that if they have nothing to hide, they have nothing to fear.

Zuboff says: 'If you have nothing to hide, you are nothing. What drives you as a person? What motivates you? What are your dreams? It is about who you are as a human being, your inner motives.' (Lenters, 2019).

In *Inequality.com: Power, poverty and the digital divide*, O'Hara and Stevens point out that a more accurate response would be to say: '

If you keep within the law, and the government keeps within the law, and its employees keep within the law, and the computer holding the database doesn't screw up, and the system is carefully designed according to well-understood software engineering principles and maintained properly, and the government doesn't scrimp on the outlay, and all the data is entered carefully, and the police are adequately trained to use the system, and the system isn't hacked into, and your identity isn't stolen, and the local hardware functions well, you have nothing to fear.

(O'Hara and Stevens, 2006, 251-2)

The nothing to hide, nothing to fear argument is bogus. It conveniently overlooks the power and control dimension. As Cardinal Richelieu said in the famous quotation 'If one would give me six lines written by the hand of the most honest man, I would find something in them to have him hanged'.

1.3.3   The functional relationship of privacy with other values

Privacy has a functional relationship with other values and furthers the existence of a free society. Any limitations on privacy places those values (such as liberty, autonomy - including moral autonomy - selfhood, human relations, equal treatment and trust) at risk. Without them our liberal democratic society will lose its foundation.

Are we really willing to relinquish privacy and a host of other values in the name of security? (Solove, 2011, 2) says that 'the debate between privacy and security has been framed incorrectly with the tradeoff between these values understood as an all-or-nothing proposition. But protecting privacy need not be fatal to security measures, it merely demands oversight and regulation'. The reasons why the security side of the argument normally wins out over privacy goes back to the complex nature of privacy. As Solove points out, 'security interests are readily understood, for life and limb are at stake, while privacy rights remain more abstract and vague'.

1.3.4   Protecting library user privacy is not merely an issue of data protection

The six data protection principles (GDPR Article 5) require that personal data shall be:

1 processed lawfully, fairly and in a transparent manner
2 collected for specified, explicit and legitimate purposes
3 adequate, relevant and not excessive
4 accurate and, where necessary, kept up to date
5 kept for no longer than necessary
6 processed in a manner that ensures appropriate security.

However, it is important to make clear that data protection is not the same as privacy. The Charter of Fundamental Rights of the European Union has distinct and separate articles covering privacy (Article 7) and personal data (Article 8).

So the Charter of Fundamental Rights clearly splits out and separates data protection from privacy.

If we as library and information professionals were to focus exclusively on data protection we would be in danger of failing to properly protect the privacy of library users. Data protection deals with the informational privacy of natural persons, whereas scholars[1] have over the last 50 years or more developed a list of distinct and separate types of privacy, with Koops et al. (2017) identifying eight specific types.

The right to data protection and the right to be forgotten are both examples of *procedural rights*, whereas the right to identity and the right to privacy are both examples of *substantive rights*. Procedural rights cover the rules, methods and conditions through which the substantive rights are enforced. Procedural requirements include things like transparency, accessibility and proportionality.

Data protection and privacy differ both formally and substantially, although there are overlaps:

- Data protection is broader, because it applies automatically each time personal data is processed, whereas privacy is only triggered if there has been an interference with one's right to privacy.
- Data protection is narrower, because it only deals with the processing of personal data, whereas privacy applies to the processing of personal and non-personal data where it affects one's privacy.
- The proportionality tests for the right to privacy and the right to the protection of personal data may well diverge.

> The distinction between PII and non-PII is not just in need of adjustment, but must be completely abandoned because the list of potential PII (or quasi-identifiers) 'will never stop growing until it includes everything'.
>
> (Rubinstein and Hartzog, 2016)

Another key difference between data protection and privacy is the way in which data protection has the individual as its focus, making it difficult to represent the interests of groups of individuals – such as minorities or vulnerable groups – who may suffer privacy harms at the group level. The titles of the data protection legislation reflect the focus on the individual:

- Directive 95/46/EC on the protection of individuals with regard to the processing of personal data and on the free movement of such data (now replaced by the GDPR)
- Council of Europe Convention of 28 January 1981 for the Protection of Individuals with regard to the Automatic Processing of Personal Data

- Regulation 2016/679 on the protection of natural persons with regard to the processing of personal data and on the free movement of such data (GDPR).

It is true, though, that Article 80 of the GDPR does deal with representation of data subjects, and allows not-for-profit bodies, organisations or associations to act on behalf of individuals.

1.3.5   The different types of privacy

Koops et al. (2017) identify eight distinct types of privacy, and in Table 1.1 I have put together library examples for each of Koops' privacy types.

Table 1.1 *Library examples of the different types of privacy using the privacy types of Koops et al. (2017)*

Koops' privacy type	Library examples
Bodily privacy	The use of facial recognition to identify library users (Lambert, 2016)
Spatial privacy	Co-location of libraries with other council functions such as customer service centres, or locating libraries alongside community-focused amenities (Freeman, 2016)
Communicational privacy	A patron uses the library to access his e-mail and leaves a printout of an e-mail of a very personal nature on the public printer at closing time (Balas, 2005)
Proprietary privacy	Disclosure of private facts could impact upon a library user's reputation. For example, if the librarian were to disclose the names of users who have run up the highest unpaid fines; or if they were to disclose who had been reading books about drug addiction.
Intellectual privacy	Installing a Tor exit relay in a library in order to enable autonomy of internet use, to protect the seeking of information online and ensuring intellectual privacy (Siegel, 2016)
Decisional privacy	The 'chilling effect' of suspecting that one's internet browsing data or book borrowing data is being monitored could impact on one's freedom to make important choices. Examples would include a teenager wanting to consult material on having an abortion; or a middle-aged man wanting to read up about divorce.
Associational privacy	The footage from the library's CCTV cameras being used to determine who a particular library user is meeting.

Continued

Table 1.1 *Continued*

Koops' privacy type	Library examples
Behavioural privacy	A mother and her 10-year-old son went to their local library. The boy was standing in a locked stall in the library's toilets when he saw a mobile phone peering over the divider. The mother reported the man to library staff. He was subsequently arrested and charged with video voyeurism (Marr, 2018)

Conspicuous by its absence from this list of eight privacy types is informational privacy. For Koops et al., informational privacy is an overlay which should be placed across the eight privacy types. Every privacy scenario will involve informational privacy to a greater or lesser degree, along with one or more of the eight privacy types.

Koops et al. (2017, 556) say that 'scholars often conceptualise privacy in negative or positive terms, or connect privacy to the concepts of negative and positive freedom - frequently referred to as "freedom from" and "freedom to", respectively'.

They developed a conceptual model in which the eight different types of privacy that they identify are grouped into two different categories.

First, there are those which place their emphasis on *freedom from* (being let alone):

- bodily privacy
- spatial privacy
- communicational privacy
- proprietary privacy.

Then there are those which place their emphasis on *freedom to* (self-development):

- intellectual privacy
- decisional privacy
- associational privacy
- behavioural privacy.

A library user's freedom from intrusions on the functioning of their mind could be seen more positively as the freedom to exercise their mind. This could, for example, translate into that particular user's freedom to read books or articles, or browse web pages, on topics such as divorce or abortion.

Warren and Brandeis (1890) presented one of the earliest and most succinctly enunciated definitions of privacy as 'the right to be let alone', which places the emphasis on the *freedom from*.

1.4   The types of personal data collected by libraries

Libraries may collect the following types of personal data:

- circulation records:
  - items borrowed
  - items returned
  - items reserved
  - overdue books
  - interlibrary loans
- billing records (such as for lost or damaged items, or overdue items)
- book recommendations
- online catalogue and database searches
- alerts
- saved searches
- personalisation (such as tailoring an online database around one's interests)
- transaction logs
- computer browsing history
- e-mail and web chat communications
- user records:
  - current user profiles
  - lapsed/former users
- electronic reserves/course readings
- rating, tagging and commenting on articles.

Library users may not realise just how much data is gathered about their library activity when they interact with library services. For example, when looking for an article using a library discovery service, everything is recorded with great granularity:

- authentication method used
- search terms used
- length of time spent looking at each page
- what is downloaded.

Public use of libraries reveals a great number of private details:

- communication (e-mail and social media)
- online banking and e-commerce

- research and browsing
- applying for jobs and benefits.

For example, Derbyshire Libraries had an initiative to provide work and money help online from their library branches.[2] They promoted this by saying that local libraries can help with many work and money issues, including: searching and applying for jobs online; using the find-a-job website or e-mailing your CV; and using a computer to apply online for benefits.

By its very nature, this initiative inevitably meant that library staff were processing personally identifiable information about their users.

1.5   The privacy of the library as a public space

Sturges, Iliffe and Dearnley (2001) recognise that 'The library, whether public, academic or institutional, is both a communal and a private space: a paradox that has always contained a certain potential for tensions.' They acknowledge that privacy is even less possible in the digital library than it is in the print library.

Campbell and Cowan (2016) acknowledge that privacy can have a paradoxical relation to the public sphere. They cite Keizer (2012), who suggests that individuals frequently move into the public sphere not to sacrifice their privacy, but to retain it. Indeed, in an analysis of a court decision that grappled with the question of privacy in public places, Keizer writes of 'the number of people whose very act of stepping out the front door represents a "subjective expectation of privacy" – because the public sphere is the only place where they can have a reasonable hope of finding it'.

As they say, the 'library occupies a position of significant though paradoxical importance: its status as a public place makes it an ideal place in which to experience genuine privacy'. Referring to the concept of 'open inquiry', they say that it 'consists of the freedom to inquire, unrestricted by familial, communal, or tribal obligations'. Indeed Keizer suggests that 'The public sphere may well be the most important factor in an individual's quest to use information sources to explore and articulate a sexual identity with a reasonable expectation of privacy.'

The idea of open inquiry only being achieved in the privacy of the public sphere may seem like a contradiction in terms. But a teenager exploring their sexuality might well turn to the library on the basis that they crave the privacy offered by (the library as) a public space. Curry (2005) cites Steven Joyce, whose dissertation notes that many youths still living at home may be reluctant to undertake web research on their home computer, preferring instead the anonymity and safety of the public library. A teenager may well prefer the anonymity of the library over and above the lack of privacy at home where one of their parents may peer around their bedroom door unexpectedly to see what they are up to and what they are looking at on the web.

Floridi (2014, 107) cites a Pew Internet & American Life project on 'Teens, Privacy and Online Social Networks'. For youth, 'privacy' is not a singular variable. Different types of information are seen as more or less private; choosing what to conceal or reveal is an intense and ongoing process. Rather than viewing a distinct division between 'private' and 'public', young people view social contexts as multiple and overlapping. Indeed, the very distinction between 'public' and 'private' is problematic for many young people, who tend to view privacy in more nuanced ways, conceptualising internet spaces as 'semi-public' or making distinctions between different groups of 'friends'.

The question inevitably arises as to whether one can have a reasonable expectation of privacy in a public place. In a landmark 1967 case, Katz v. United States (389 US 347), the US Supreme Court found that a warrantless police recording device attached to the outside of a telephone booth violated the Fourth Amendment's protection against unreasonable searches and seizures. This protection had formerly been construed primarily in cases involving intrusion into a physical place, but in Katz (at 351) the justices famously held that the Fourth Amendment 'protects people, not places'.

Notes

1   Finn, Wright and Friedewald (2013); Clarke (1997); Pedersen (1979; 1997); Westin (1967); Koops et al. (2017).
2   www.derbyshire.gov.uk/leisure/libraries/services/work-and-money-help/work-and-money-help-online-from-your-local-library.aspx.

CHAPTER 2

How privacy is regulated in the UK

In English law there is no overarching cause of action for 'invasion of privacy' (Wainwright v. Home Office, 2003). Instead, anyone bringing an action relating to breach of privacy would rely on the rights in the European Convention on Human Rights or the English law of confidence.

The legislative regime in the UK for privacy consists of a number of components:

- UK legislation in the form of Acts and Statutory Instruments
- international commitments through agreements such as the European Convention on Human Rights
- relevant case law.

One could also add 'soft law', quasi-legal instruments which do not have any legally binding force. The term 'soft law' could encompass a wide range of instruments of a different nature and functions which cannot easily be contained within a single formula or description. These include standards, guidelines, codes of ethics and professional values.

2.1   Legislation

Privacy and data protection are not direct equivalents of one another. Data protection relates to informational privacy, but privacy embraces much more than just the informational component (see also sections 1.3.4 and 1.3.5 in the previous chapter). The complex nature of privacy is reflected in the fact that privacy legislation extends beyond the obvious areas of data protection, human rights, and surveillance. It also reaches into areas such as terrorism, voyeurism, revenge porn and the common law on breach of confidence.

The way in which data and privacy are protected has changed significantly over the past few decades. There was no international legal instrument governing data protection until the Council of Europe's 1981 Convention for the Protection of Individuals with Regard to Automatic Processing of Personal Data. The UK's first Data Protection Act received royal assent in 1984. This was superseded by the Data Protection Act of 1998, which implemented the EU's 1995 Data Protection Directive (95/46/EC). And these were in turn replaced by the Data Protection Act 2018 and the GDPR respectively.

2.1.1   Data protection
Data Protection Act 2018
The Data Protection Act 2018 provides a comprehensive legal framework for data protection in the UK in accordance with the GDPR. It contains strong sanctions for malpractice. The Act gives people more control over the use of their data, and provides new rights to move or delete personal data. The DPA 2018 specifies or defines certain aspects of the GDPR in relation to the UK such as the role of the ICO and it provides exemptions to the GDPR notably to law enforcement and intelligence services.

General Data Protection Regulation (Regulation (EU) 2016/679)
GDPR consists of a robust privacy framework which aims to give more control to individuals over their personal data. It governs the processing of personal data by data controllers and data processors.

The GDPR contains the bulk of the UK's data protection legislation. For example, if a data subject makes a Subject Access Request (SAR) it comes under Article 15 of the GDPR.

Privacy and Electronic Communications Regulations 2003 (as amended)
The Regulations apply to all organisations and individuals that send direct marketing messages by electronic means, including by an automated calling system. They cover:

- cookies and other internet tracking software
- electronic marketing mail, including e-mail, SMS text, picture and voice messages
- telephone marketing
- fax marketing
- automated calling systems, transmitting sounds that are not live speech.

The Regulations implemented directive 2002/58/EC in the UK. The European Union are in the process of replacing the directive with a Regulation (see COM (2017) 10 final).

At the time of writing, the UK are in the process of leaving the European Union. Nevertheless, the UK's data protection laws will continue to be closely aligned with those of the EU, as this is essential for trade within the European Economic Area to be as frictionless as possible.

2.1.2   Human rights

The European Convention on Human Rights (ECHR)

The Convention is an international treaty by the Council of Europe to protect human rights and fundamental freedoms. It established the European Court of Human Rights to enforce the Convention.

Under the European Convention on Human Rights (ECHR) privacy is recognised as a human right based around 'the respect for private and family life'. Article 8 of the ECHR protects four things: (1) private life; (2) family life; (3) home; and (4) correspondence/communications.

The law has to find a balance between competing human rights. There are two parts of the ECHR which regularly compete against each other. Article 8 deals with the right to respect for private and family life, home and correspondence. It often competes with Article 10, which covers freedom of expression. Indeed, most breach of privacy cases relating to the publication or disclosure of material have to balance Articles 8 and 10 when deciding if the material should be considered confidential or whether it is in the public interest to disclose such information.

Both the right to privacy (Article 8) and the right to freedom of expression (Article 10) are qualified, not absolute, rights.

The text of Article 8 (the right to privacy) qualifies it by saying:

> There shall be no interference by a public authority with the exercise of this right except such as is in accordance with the law and is necessary in a democratic society in the interests of

> – national security
> – public safety
> – the economic well-being of the country
> – the prevention of disorder or crime
> – the protection of health or morals, or
> – the protection of the rights and freedoms of others.

Under Article 10 of the ECHR everyone has the right to freedom of expression, which includes freedom to hold opinions and to receive and impart information and ideas without interference by public authority and regardless of frontiers. As with Article 8, Article 10 is not an absolute right. The right to freedom of expression is qualified in the following manner:

> The exercise of these freedoms, since it carries with it duties and responsibilities, may be subject to such formalities, conditions, restrictions or penalties as are prescribed by law and are necessary in a democratic society, in the interests of

– national security,
– territorial integrity
– public safety
– the prevention of disorder or crime
– the protection of health or morals
– the protection of the reputation or rights of others
– preventing the disclosure of information received in confidence
– maintaining the authority and impartiality of the judiciary.

The Human Rights Act 1998

The Act applies the ECHR in the UK. It is composed of a series of sections that have the effect of codifying the protections in the Convention into UK law and, as a result, has made the Convention rights enforceable in UK courts. Individuals can file human rights cases in domestic courts, rather than having to go to Strasbourg to argue their case.

2.1.3   Surveillance

Investigatory Powers Act 2016

The Investigatory Powers Act provides an updated framework for the use (by the security and intelligence agencies, law enforcement and other public authorities) of investigatory powers to obtain communications and communications data. These powers cover the interception of communications, the retention and acquisition of communications data, and equipment interference for obtaining communications and other data.

The term 'communications data' includes the 'who', 'when', 'where', and 'how' of a communication but not the content, i.e. what was said or written. The legal definition of 'communications data' can be found in section 262 (5) of the IPA 2016.

By emphasising the point that 'communications data' refers to the information about data, rather than the contents of the data itself, people try to reassure those who are concerned about their privacy. But this sort of metadata can be retrieved from bulk datasets and, when taken in aggregate, it can tell far more about a person than the contents ever would. Metadata in aggregate is a form of content.

Regulation of Investigatory Powers Act 2000

The Regulation of Investigatory Powers Act 2000 (RIPA) regulates the powers of public bodies to carry out surveillance and investigation. It governs the use of covert surveillance such as bugs, video surveillance and interception of private communications (such as phone calls and e-mails) and even undercover agents ('covert human intelligence sources').

2.1.4   Terrorism

Terrorism Act 2000

The Act reformed and extended previous counter-terrorism legislation, and put it largely on a permanent basis. Part VI (Miscellaneous) of the Act provides a number of offences, including possessing information for terrorist purposes (section 103). It is a defence to prove that a person had a reasonable excuse for the collection of such information.

Terrorism Act 2006

Under section 1 of the Terrorism Act 2006 it is a criminal offence to publish, or cause another to publish, a statement that is likely to be understood as direct or indirect encouragement or inducement to commit, prepare or instigate acts of terrorism.

Under section 2 of the Terrorism Act 2006 librarians run the risk of committing the offence of 'dissemination of terrorist publications'. The term 'publication' refers to matter to be read, listened to, looked at or watched. So this isn't just confined to books.

CILIP's guide to User Privacy in Libraries (CILIP, 2011, 12–13) states that CILIP 'does not endorse the use of filtering especially for adult users but recognises that a number of libraries do use filtering systems especially if it is required by their parent institution', whilst acknowledging the appropriateness of discouraging users from viewing illegal sites such as those associated with terrorism.

A student at Staffordshire University who was studying for a master's degree in terrorism and security was spotted by security guards in the university library reading a book on terrorism studies. He is said to have felt unsettled and looking over his shoulder after the incident (Sherriff, 2015). In light of the counter-terrorism legislation it is important to ensure that staff have the right guidance and training.

PREVENT strategy

The UK Government's PREVENT Strategy and the Counter-Terrorism and Security Act 2015 places a duty on local authorities in England, Wales and Scotland, and the people who work for them, to spot early warning signs of terrorist sympathy, and report individuals to the police. The 2015 Act requires local authorities to develop plans to safeguard individuals from getting involved in terrorism.

Internet-specific measures to be taken in order to address the threat of radicalisation online might include:

- limiting access to harmful content online in specific sectors or premises (notably schools, public libraries and other public buildings)
- use of filtering software
- institutions monitoring e-mails in an attempt to comply with the Counter-Terrorism and Security Act 2015.

One of the UK's most prestigious universities warned students and staff that their e-mails might be retained and monitored as part of the government's PREVENT programme to stop radicalisation on campuses (Weale, 2017).

2.1.5   Voyeurism
The Sexual Offences Act 2003

Section 67 of The Sexual Offences Act 2003 contains an offence of voyeurism. However, until it was amended by The Voyeurism (Offences) Act 2019, the 2003 Act did not adequately protect people from upskirting (the act of covertly photographing underneath someone's clothing without their consent).

The way that section 67 was worded meant that the taking of intimate videos without consent would often fall outside the scope of the offence, even when done for sexual gratification. The offence required the person to be doing a private act, or to be in a place such as a lavatory or a changing room where some degree of exposure or nudity may occur but where one could reasonably expect privacy. Neither of these conditions was fulfilled when the victim is fully dressed in a public place, for example where they are on public transport or at a music festival.

The Voyeurism (Offences) Act 2019

The Voyeurism (Offences) Act 2019 inserted a new section 67A into The Sexual Offences Act 2003.

A person commits an offence if they operate equipment beneath the clothing of another person with the intention of enabling themselves or another person to observe that person's genitals or buttocks (whether exposed or covered with underwear), in circumstances where the genitals, buttocks or underwear would not otherwise be visible, and does so without that person's consent and without them reasonably believing that the person has consented, where they do so for one of the following purposes: obtaining sexual gratification; or humiliating, alarming or distressing that person.

A person guilty of an offence under this section could be imprisoned for a term not exceeding two years, or face a fine or both.

Criminal Justice and Courts Act 2015

Sections 33-35 and Schedule 8 of the Act created an offence which criminalises the malicious disclosure of photographs or films (such as revenge porn - 'the sharing of private, sexual materials, either photos or videos, of another person without their consent and with the purpose of causing embarrassment or distress. The images are sometimes accompanied by personal information about the subject, including their full name, address and links to their social media profiles' (Ministry of Justice, 2015). The disclosure must take place without the consent of at least one of those featured in the picture disclosed and with the intent of causing that person distress. The offence carries a two-year maximum custodial penalty.

2.2   Contracts

Data protection and privacy issues are regularly subject to contract law. In a library context, this would include licence agreements with vendors, or contractual agreements with third-party data processors.

One of the situations where processing of personal data is considered to be 'lawful' is where handling the data is necessary to fulfil a contract that citizens are party to (GDPR Article 6 1(b)).

GDPR requires organisations to have written contracts with any supplier that processes library users' personal data (GDPR Article 28).

Although most users are unlikely to peruse the terms of licence agreements that libraries have with their vendors, making the terms readily available is a necessary (though not sufficient) condition for respecting the autonomy of patrons and thus for supporting the quality-of-agency facet of intellectual freedom.

Even if users have ready access to all of the licence agreements that their local library service has with its vendors, they would be unlikely to take the time and trouble to read through the entire wording of each of the agreements. It needs to be put into the wider context of the privacy policies governing websites in general. One study estimated that in order to read all website privacy policies encountered in one year, it would take 201 hours - equalling US$3,534 - per American internet user (McDonald and Cranor, 2008, 562).

'Libraries should ensure that contract terms pertaining to data collection, data sharing with third parties, and monitoring and disciplinary actions for unauthorised use are transparent to users' (Rubel and Zhang, 2015, 445). If librarians want their users to make an informed choice about whether or not to use services that the library offers through external vendors, they can help them by providing an explanation as to personal data those services collect, the reasons for doing so and whether it is shared in turn with any of the vendor's third parties. For users to be able to give meaningful and informed consent, such explanations need to be given in clear, succinct, and unambiguous terms (see Figure 2.1 on the next page).

Privacy implications of services provided through external vendors

Is it always clear to library users when they are being directed to a service offered by an external vendor?

Do you make clear to library users that the site is governed by the vendor's own privacy policy?

Do you make it easy for library users to be able to access the vendor's privacy policy?

Do you help users by summarising the key points of the vendor's privacy policy?

In other words, are the users in a position to make an informed choice as to whether or not to use the service offered by that particular vendor?

Figure 2.1 *Privacy implications of services provided through external vendors*

2.2.1 Third countries where there is no adequacy decision

A 'third country' is a country other than the EU member states and the three additional EEA countries (Norway, Iceland and Liechtenstein) that have adopted a national law implementing the GDPR.

In the absence of an adequacy decision (where the EU has decided that the third country ensures an adequate level of protection of personal data), data controllers or processors should take measures to compensate for the lack of data protection in a third country by way of appropriate safeguards for the data subject (GDPR Article 46). Such appropriate safeguards may consist of:

- making use of binding corporate rules
- standard data protection clauses adopted by the Commission
- standard data protection clauses adopted by a supervisory authority or
- contractual clauses authorised by a supervisory authority.

2.3   Guidelines
CILIP

CILIP produced a document titled *User Privacy in Libraries: guidelines for the reflective practitioner* (CILIP, 2011), although these guidelines were last revised in 2011. Because of their age, they do not reflect the significant changes to the UK's data protection laws which occurred in 2018.

A more recent CILIP document is *Leading the Way: a guide to privacy for public library staff* (Charillon, 2018).

American Library Association

The American Library Association has produced a range of guidelines covering topics such as privacy as it relates to library management systems, library websites and the use of networked devices:

- *Library Privacy Guidelines for E-Book Lending and Digital Content Vendors* (American Library Association, 2015)
- *Library Privacy Guidelines for Data Exchange Between Networked Devices and Services* (American Library Association, 2016a)
- *Library Privacy Guidelines for Library Management Systems* (American Library Association, 2016b)
- *Library Privacy Guidelines for Library Websites, OPACs, and Discovery Services* (American Library Association, 2016c)
- *Library Privacy Guidelines for Public Access Computers and Networks* (American Library Association, 2016d)
- *Library Privacy Guidelines for Students in K-12 Schools* (American Library Association, 2016e)
- *Suggested Guidelines: how to respond to law enforcement requests for library records and user information* (American Library Association, 2017)

NISO

- *NISO Consensus Principles on Users' Digital Privacy in Library, Publisher, and Software-Provider Systems* (NISO, 2015).

2.4   Standards

EN 16570 and EN 16571 are the two standards which are designed to implement the European Commission's Mandate M/436 on RFID privacy (European Commission. Enterprise and Industry Directorate-General, 2008).

The worldwide Payment Card Industry Data Security Standard (PCIDSS) has 12 high-level requirements, falling into six categories:

1 Build and maintain a secure network.
2 Protect cardholder data.
3 Maintain a vulnerability management programme.
4 Implement strong access control measures.
5 Regularly monitor and test networks.
6 Maintain an information security policy.

Table 2.1 *British and International Standards*

Standard number	Title
ISO-IEC 27018 2019	Information technology – Security techniques – Code of practice for protection of personally identifiable information (PII) in public clouds acting as PII processors (Ex Libris was the first vendor in the industry to adopt this globally recognised standard for cloud privacy)

Table 2.1 *Continued*

Standard number	Title
ISO/IEC 18000-6:2010	Information technology – Radio frequency identification for item management – Part 6: Parameters for air interface communications at 860 MHz to 960 MHz
BS 10012:2017+ A1:2018	Data protection. Specification for a personal information management system
BS EN 16570:2014	Information technology. Notification of RFID. The information sign and additional information to be provided by operators of RFID application systems
BS EN 16571:2014	Information technology. RFID privacy impact assessment process
ISO 15489-1:2016	Information and documentation – Records management – Part 1: Concepts and principles Recognised professional certifications such as ISC2 Certified Information System Security Professional (CISSP), ISACA Certified Information Security Auditor, IAPP Certified Privacy Professional, and others. Also, they should maintain an information security program that is certified to the ISO/IEC 27001 standard, an international benchmark.
ISO/IEC 27005:2018	Information technology – Security techniques – Information security risk management
ISO/IEC 27000 family	Information security management systems ISO/IEC 27001 is the best-known standard in the family providing requirements for an information security management system (ISMS).
ISO/IEC 15693-1:2018	Cards and security devices for personal identification – Contactless vicinity objects – Part 1: Physical characteristics
ISO/IEC 27002:2013	Information technology – Security techniques – Code of practice for information security controls
ISO/IEC 27018:2014	Information technology – Security techniques – Code of practice for protection of personally identifiable information (PII) in public clouds acting as PII processors
ISO/IEC 29100:2011	Information technology – Security techniques – Privacy framework
ISO/IEC 19086-1:2016(en)	Information technology – Cloud computing – Service level agreement (SLA) framework – Part 1: Overview and concepts

2.5   Ethical/professional values

2.5.1   Professional ethics

Shachaf (2005) undertook a comparative content analysis of the codes of ethics proposed by professional associations in 28 countries. She found that 'the most frequently identified principles were professional development, integrity, confidentiality or privacy, and free and equal access to information'.

CILIP's ethical framework (CILIP, 2018a) says that:

> As an ethical information professional I make a commitment to uphold, promote and defend . . . (A6) the confidentiality of information provided by clients or users and the right of all individuals to privacy.

The clarifying notes which accompany the ethical framework (CILIP, 2018b) elaborate on this by saying that:

> As recognised by IFLA in its *Code of Ethics for Librarians and Other Information Workers*, [Garcia-Febo et al., 2012] library and information professionals should respect personal privacy, and the protection of personal data necessarily shared between individuals and institutions. The relationship between the library and the user is one of confidentiality and appropriate measures should be taken to ensure that user data is not shared beyond the original transaction without their consent.

CILIP's 2018 ethical framework replaced its previous set of ethical principles and code of professional practice. Those older documents said more about the privacy of library users than the new ethical framework does. The old principles stated that: 'The conduct of members should be characterised by the following general principles and values . . .'. Point 8 of the 12 that are listed in the earlier set of CILIP ethical principles refers to: 'Respect for confidentiality and privacy in dealing with information users'. Meanwhile the old CILIP code of professional practice also includes several points about confidentiality:

- Under 'Responsibilities to information and its users' it says that members should: 'Protect the confidentiality of all matters relating to information users, including their enquiries, any services to be provided, and any aspects of the users' personal circumstances or business.'
- Under 'Responsibilities to Society' it says: 'Strive to achieve an appropriate balance within the law between demands from information users, the need to respect confidentiality, the terms of their employment, the public good and the responsibilities outlined in this Code.'

The American Library Association recently added a new provision to their Library Bill of Rights:

> All people, regardless of origin, age, background, or views, possess a right to privacy and confidentiality in their library use. Libraries should advocate for, educate about, and protect people's privacy, safeguarding all library use data, including personally identifiable information (Article VII).
>
> (Caldwell-Stone, 2019)

2.5.2   Michael Gorman's eight enduring values of librarianship

Privacy is one of our professional values as information professionals. Michael Gorman, in *Our Enduring Values* (2000) and *Our Enduring Values Revisited* (2015), lists privacy as one of his eight enduring values:

1 stewardship
2 service
3 intellectual freedom
4 rationalism
5 literacy and learning
6 equity of access
7 privacy:
     a) ensuring the confidentiality of records of library use
     b) overcoming technological invasions of library use
8 democracy.

Gorman wrote *Our Enduring Values* in the 1990s, and it was published by the ALA in 2000. Fifteen years later, he followed it up with *Our Enduring Values Revisited*. The update was prompted by the societal, economic and technological changes and the changing nature of library user privacy protection which have impacted on the work of libraries in the period since the original work was published.

Amongst the trends and changes that Gorman reflected on was 'the death of privacy', and the assault on privacy which results from technological change.

2.6   Case law

The legal system in England is known as a *common law system*, that is one in which case law plays an important role. In most of continental Europe and parts of Latin America they have a different legal system, known as a *civil law system*, where the law is written down in statutes in a very logical and organised - codified - way across all of the subject areas. In the civil law system, case law does not have the same significance that it does in the common law system. In civil law systems, case law is merely illustrative. They place more importance on commentaries from professors and judges published in books and journal articles than they do on case law.

2.6.1   Breach of confidence

The common law tort of breach of confidence deals with unauthorised use or disclosure of certain types of information and it provides protection for that information to be kept secret. This branch of the law is based upon the principle that a person who has obtained information in confidence should not take unfair advantage of it. The main means used to achieve this is the interim injunction (interdict in Scotland), which is an order of the court directing a party to refrain from disclosing the confidential information. A document may be considered confidential where there is:

- an obligation of non-disclosure within a particular document
- a duty in certain papers involving professional relationships
- a duty of confidence which arises where a reasonable individual may determine that a document contains confidential information.

2.6.2   English legal cases on privacy

There are a number of legal cases which help to clarify where people have a right to privacy. There is some case law directly relevant to privacy in libraries and bookshops, but this is mainly from the USA rather than from the UK.

The case of **Murray v. Big Pictures [2008] EWCA Civ 446** helps to clarify where one would have a reasonable expectation of privacy. Paragraph 36 of the judgment says that:

the question of whether there is a reasonable expectation of privacy is a broad one, which takes account of all the circumstances of the case. They include:

- The attributes of the claimant;
- The nature of the activity in which the claimant was engaged;
- The place in which it was happening;
- The nature and purpose of the intrusion;
- The absence of consent; and
- Whether it was known or could be inferred;
- The effect on the claimant; and
- The circumstances in which and the purposes for which the information came into the hands of the [person using it].

2.6.3   American legal cases on privacy in bookshops and libraries

Most legal cases dealing with privacy in relation to libraries, bookshops and newsletter publishers are American rather than British.

It is important to stress the fact that the way in which the law protects patron privacy does differ between the UK and the USA; and also that America's legal system consists of the law of each state as well as federal law.

Nevertheless, I have picked out a selection of American legal cases on these topics, because they wrestle with the issues under consideration by this book.

In **Quad/Graphics v. S Adirondack 174 Misc. 2d 291 (1997) 664 N.Y.S. 2d 225** the question of access to library usage records was considered. Southern Adirondack Library System (SALS) operated a 'Library Without Walls' (LWW) service whereby users of LWW who were in possession of a valid library card and personal ID number that had been issued by any of the SALS participating libraries could access the internet. A cadre of the employees of Quad/Graphics were accused of using the LWW feature during working hours to access the internet for personal purposes. This led to the company incurring over US$23,000 worth of long-distance phone charges, and involved the loss of 1,770 man-hours which had been devoted to personal use of the internet.

Quad/Graphics were able to identify nine 13-digit identification numbers that had been used to access the LWW feature and were seeking to establish the identity of the individuals who they had been issued to. They submitted an FOI request to the Saratoga Springs Public Library but this was rejected by the library on the basis of the information being confidential.

The court ruled in favour of the library. There wasn't a criminal complaint before the court, and if the information request had been granted it would leave the door open for similar requests, such as where a parent wishes to learn what their child is reading or viewing on the internet or by a spouse wishing to know what type of information his or her mate is viewing at the public library.

In **Tattered Cover, Inc. v. City of Thornton, 44 P. 3d 1044** the court ruled that the federal and state constitutions prevented law enforcement from finding out what books an individual purchased at Denver's Tattered Cover Bookstore, unless law enforcement could show the information is critical to a prosecution.

Chief Justice Michael L. Bender used a test to determine whether or not the information should be disclosed. The first prong of the test provided that the government must not do anything that abridges fundamental rights unless there is an appropriate connection to a compelling government interest. That connection must be direct and significant. The second prong required that there must be a 'significant connection' between the criminal investigation and the information being sought. Finally, 'officials must exhaust [other] alternatives before resorting to techniques that implicate fundamental expressive rights of bookstores and their customers'.

In **Brown v. Johnston 328 N.W. 2d 510 (Iowa 1983)** it was held that the statutory section governing confidentiality of library records (Iowa Code chapter 68A) did not prevent execution of the prosecutor's *subpoena duces tecum* requiring the custodian of library records to appear and present all records of persons who have checked out certain books, and that the patron's right to privacy was overridden by the State's interest in well-founded criminal charges and fair administration of justice.

The request for library records related to a long list of titles dealing mainly with witchcraft and related topics. The ruling stated that 'Even if we assume . . . that a library patron's privilege exists, based upon the patron's right of privacy, it is only a qualified privilege. We must weight the effect of forced disclosure of these records against the societal need for the information.'

In **Doe v. Gonzales 546 US 1301** (the case of 'the Connecticut Four') the applicants - a member of the American Library Association referred to as 'John Doe', the American Civil Liberties Union and the American Civil Liberties Union Foundation - brought suit in district court, alleging that the non-disclosure provision set forth in 18 U. S. C. §2709(c) violated their First Amendment right to freedom of speech.

Section 2709 of the USA PATRIOT Act 2001 authorised the FBI to 'request the name, address, length of service, and local and long-distance toll billing records of a person or entity' if the FBI asserts in writing that the information requested is relevant to an investigation against international terrorism or clandestine intelligence activities'.

The information was requested in the form of a National Security Letter (NSL). A director of the Library Connection (referred to in the case as John Doe) had been presented with an NSL demanding disclosure of 'any and all subscriber information, billing information[,]and access logs of any person or entity'.

Recipients of an NSL are prohibited from disclosing the fact that they have been asked for information. John Doe argued that the gagging order was an unlawful prior restraint on free speech. The district court had concluded that the prohibition on disclosure was permissible only if it satisfied strict scrutiny.

The court could find nothing to suggest that the government had a compelling interest in preventing disclosure of Doe's identity.

In June 2006 George Christian, Executive Director of the Library Connection, was able to identify himself as the recipient of the NSL, following the lifting of the PATRIOT Act gag order.

In **Lubin v. Agora Inc., 882 A.2d 833 (Md. Ct. App. 2005)** Maryland's court of appeals denied the state Securities Commissioner the right to subpoena the publisher of an internet newsletter for its list of current and potential subscribers. The commissioner was seeking the information as a result of a customer complaint indicating that the publisher of an internet newsletter was acting as an investment adviser without proper state registration. The circuit court in Baltimore County enforced the subpoenas, but the court of appeals reversed that decision, relying in large part upon the well-accepted First Amendment precedent that 'the government has no greater right to inquire into an individual's choice of reading materials than it does to inquire into an individual's choice of associates'. The court found that the commissioner had failed to show a sufficient nexus between the investigation into the defendant's activities and the demand for the subscriber lists.

In **United States v. Rumly, 345 U.S. 41 (1953)** the respondent was secretary of an organisation which, among other things, engaged in the sale of books of a political nature. He refused to disclose to a committee of Congress the names of those who made bulk purchases of these books for further distribution, and was convicted under R.S. § 102, as amended, which provides penalties for refusal to give testimony or to produce relevant papers 'upon any matter' under congressional inquiry.

It was held that the committee was without the power to exact the information sought from the respondent.

Justice Douglas observed, 'Once the government can demand of a publisher the names of the purchasers of his publications . . . [f]ear of criticism goes with every person into the bookstall . . . [and] inquiry will be discouraged.'

CHAPTER 3

Practical examples of privacy issues arising in a library context

Library and information professionals will naturally want to protect the privacy of their users. But how realistic is that aspiration?

- For most information professionals privacy is only one of a multitude of legal and ethical considerations for them to comply with.
- They are highly unlikely to have the luxury of being able to focus exclusively on privacy and confidentiality issues when evaluating the services their libraries offer.
- How many library staff will have read and be fully familiar with the wording of all of the contracts that the library service has in place with vendors and partners?

There is also the question of how realistic it is for library users to be able to protect the privacy of their personal data:

- Do library users know how the various technologies used by the library work and their information security vulnerabilities?
- Are library users likely to know about any technological measures in place to ensure that personal data is processed in a secure manner?
- Does the library offer training to users which covers privacy, such as sessions about how to stay safe online?
- Are library users familiar with the library's privacy policy?
- Do library users always know when they are being directed to a service provided by an external vendor, governed by that vendor's privacy policy?
- Do library users fully understand the implications of the privacy policies of both the library itself and of each of the vendors that the library uses?

If the answer to these questions is NO, how can library users make an informed choice as to whether they wish to entrust the library with their personal data?

Libraries rely on the internet in order to be able to provide a full range of services. It is important to reflect on the implications of this wider environment:

- tech companies that make information public by default
- people tending not to routinely change the default privacy settings
- companies that give themselves the freedom to change their terms and conditions (T&Cs) at any time
- T&Cs that are not negotiated
- cloud computing providing an opportunity for governments to get at our personal data
- governments that don't want information providers to tell users when their data has been accessed
- American libraries resorting to use of a 'warrant canary' to get around being unable to say that data has been accessed
- digital footprints and digital shadows being created and added to all the time
- the difficulty of being able to anonymise data in the face of correlation attacks
- the use of stingray fake phone masts (also known as IMSI catchers) to hoover up information from mobile devices (Griffin, 2015).

There is no way to guarantee privacy. The best we can hope for is to minimise the risk. For individual library users the question they have to ask is: 'How much effort am I willing to put into keeping my information private?' This is where library and information professionals have a role - they can help with education and awareness. They can be well attuned to the risks, be on the lookout for any vulnerabilities, and ensure that these are mitigated wherever possible. They can and should work with their vendors to ensure that privacy and confidentiality issues are adequately covered in the contracts they negotiate; and alert vendors to any information security vulnerabilities and privacy risks that they discover, so that these can be addressed as soon as they come to light.

This book aims to help library and information professionals be more privacy-aware and to be mindful of the need to protect the privacy and confidentiality of the interactions that their users have with them and with the library service as a whole.

It is important to be able to step back and look dispassionately at the way in which the library operates, to do so with fresh eyes, being sensitive to any potential privacy issues - all the more so if your library is contemplating the introduction of a new service or revamping the way in which an existing service or procedure operates. Article 35 of the GDPR requires data controllers to consider the potential privacy risks posed by new technologies:

> Where a type of processing in particular using new technologies, and taking into account the nature, scope, context and purposes of the processing, is likely to result in a high risk to the rights and freedoms of

natural persons, the controller shall, prior to the processing, carry out an assessment of the impact of the envisaged processing operations on the protection of personal data.

This chapter contains 20 specific examples of how privacy issues can and do arise in a library context. The examples come from a range of library sectors, including public libraries, academic libraries, school libraries and libraries in the corporate sector.

3.1   Self-service holds

Public and academic libraries both offer 'click and collect' services whereby users can browse through the library catalogue from the comfort of their own homes, select the item(s) that they would like to read, watch or listen to, and then choose which library they would like to use as the pick-up location. These 'click and collect' services ensure that library users are able to pick up the requested item(s) from their chosen library at a time that is convenient for them once they have been notified that it is ready for collection.

As part of this 'click and collect' facility, many libraries place the items awaiting collection in a publicly accessible area of the library so that the library user is able to pick up the item without requiring any library staff intervention. But the procedures vary from one library to another and just as the library practices vary, so too does the extent to which their actions encroach upon the privacy of library users:

- Library 1: All of the items on hold are shelved on a standalone unit in the middle of the library. Each item is wrapped in a piece of A4 paper which shows on the spine the first three letters of the user's surname and the last few digits of the user's library card number.
- Library 2: All of the items on hold are shelved in a dedicated area of the library. This area can only be reached once the user has swiped their library card, in order to open a security gate to let them enter the area in question. Each item is wrapped in a piece of A4 paper which shows on the spine the first four letters of the user's surname and the last few digits of the user's library card number.
- Library 3: The items on hold are placed on the end of a set of library shelves in alphabetical order of the requestor's surname. All of the titles are easily browseable, because there is no paper wrapped around the items. The users' full surnames are hand-written onto a slip of paper resembling a bookmark which is placed inside the book, and as their surname is written at the top of the piece of paper it is visible to anyone looking at the items awaiting collection. The requested items are placed in alphabetical order of

surname. Library users can quickly locate the item that they have come to collect.

Of the three different procedures outlined above, the one used by library 3 is the least respectful of user privacy:

- Library 3 shows the complete surname of the requestor. As some people have unusual or distinctive surnames, it is likely that in a number of cases the surname will be sufficient to identify a specific individual.
- As there is no paper wrapped around the items that have been requested, people who are simply being nosy or who possess an idle curiosity can quickly look through the titles on the reserve shelves. If they spot titles that seem quite racy, provocative, controversial or embarrassing, they can then look for the requestor's surname to see if they recognise who has asked for that particular item.

This may not seem to be a serious breach of a library user's personal data in the grand scheme of things. But before dismissing it as unimportant, there are two things you should consider:

First, whilst it may not be the most serious breach of privacy imaginable, it is dangerous to dismiss it as being of no consequence. Therein lies a slippery slope. Where do you draw the line? If librarians are to become more attuned to privacy issues, more conscious of the need to protect the confidentiality of the interactions that their users have with the library service, it requires a particular type of culture, one in which librarians are sensitive to the privacy needs of their users. They need to be able to quickly spot any procedures which may be putting user privacy at risk.

Secondly, if you are tempted to dismiss it as being of little consequence, it is important to remember that protecting the privacy of library users depends on a relationship of trust between the user and the library/librarian. And it is clear that there are library users who absolutely do see this particular scenario as being important to them. For example, a patron of the Harold Washington Library in Chicago accused them of failing to protect the privacy of their patrons. She noticed that something was amiss when she went to pick up a book she had put on reserve. She saw shelves filled with books with receipts sticking out of the pages—with the full names of the patrons who reserved the materials:

> When I came to pick it up it was sitting out in the open with my first and last name and I was very surprised' . . . I knew right away something was wrong.
>
> (De Mar, 2018)

She pointed out that book choices should be private, and called the Chicago Public Library's reserve system a 'bunch of hooey'. Questions were raised about whether library staff had made a lapse in judgement and violated the American Library Association's best practices by leaving the names of its patrons out in plain sight.

This example need not have been problematic for user privacy had a data protection impact assessment (DPIA) been conducted at the start of a project affecting personal data. DPIAs act as a tool which addresses the 'privacy by design' aspects of the GDPR. Library staff considering a project that will affect personal data such as the implementation of a new library management system need to involve their data protection team, who will help them through the DPIA process (see Chapter 10 and https://ico.org.uk/for-organisations/guide-to-data-protection/guide-to-the-general-data-protection-regulation-gdpr/accountability-and-governance/data-protection-impact-assessments).

3.2   Receipts from self-service and enquiry desk machines

Years ago retailers realised that they were putting too much information onto till receipts, notably the full credit or debit card number. Given the threat of identity fraud, they stopped displaying the complete card number, and opted instead to show only part of the number while using asterisks to mask some of the digits.

With the prevalence of self-issue machines, libraries need to think carefully about the information that is printed out on transaction receipts. Three examples of the information shown on receipts are given in Figures 3.1 to 3.3 on the next page. The first two examples are based on the data appearing on receipts issued by one public library authority, while the third example is based on the receipt format used by a university library. The example in Figure 3.1 is a sample receipt from a self-service machine. The example in Figure 3.2 is a sample receipt issued at the same library's enquiry desk. Library patrons do not always have the option of using the self-service machines. If a user goes to collect an item that they have reserved, they are only able to use the self-service machines where the book is one from the authority's own library stock. Where the requested item has been borrowed from another borough, they have to go to the enquiry desk to get the book issued and the security tag de-sensitised, and are then handed a receipt of the type shown in Figure 3.2 below.

A legitimate question to ask would be 'Why is this particular library authority being inconsistent in its approach to privacy?' In the case of receipt 1 it has demonstrated how it is perfectly possible to avoid showing the user's name on the receipt; so why have they decided that on receipt 2 it is necessary to show both the user's first name and his surname?

If it is really judged necessary to include a user identifier on the receipt, wouldn't it be sufficient to put the borrower's barcode number (or part of the number) on the receipt instead of showing their full name?

The third sample receipt shown in Figure 3.3 comes from a university library service. By default, the user's name is shown on issue receipts generated by the self-service machine.

Nowheresville Library
Returned Items 23/01/2019 09:53
Item Title
....
....
Heads you win
Called to account: how corporate
bad behaviour
Defence of the realm
....
....
Thank you for returning items
www.councilname.gov.uk/libraries
Renewals (telephone number)

Figure 3.1 *Example of a self-service machine receipt 1*

ITEMS ISSUED/RENEWED
FOR Mr Joe Bloggs
ON 23/01/19 09:56:44
AT Nowheresville Library
Heads you win
30107021267830
DUE 13/02/19
1 item(s) issued

Figure 3.2 *Example from an enquiry desk machine receipt 2*

Nowheresville University Library Services
Customer name: Joe Bloggs
Customer ID: 28009020332484
Title: Words that change minds: mastering the
language of influence / Shelle Rose Charvet.
ID: 38009006234537
Due: 02-10-19
Total items: 1
25/09/2019 11:15
www.nowheresville.ac.uk/library

Figure 3.3 *Example of a self-service machine receipt 3*

Why does it matter if a user's name is shown on the receipts printed out at self-issue machines?

- Isn't it likely that users will utilise the printed slip as a bookmark, to show how far they are up to with the book?
- Isn't there a fair chance that some users will forget to remove the printed slip before returning the book to the library?
- Depending on how many books they borrowed in a single transaction, and the nature of the material being borrowed, the information on the slip could potentially be quite revealing about someone's reading habits.

This is not merely a hypothetical scenario. The author has come across numerous examples of books that he has perused in the library in which he has found discarded receipts from self-issue machines. Those receipts have shown the library users' names on them. Sometimes those receipts were issued a number of years ago. Sometimes the receipts contain long lists of items that were borrowed on a single library visit.

This is just one example of the sorts of privacy considerations that librarians should be mindful of when they introduce a new library management system, and/or new self-issue terminals. It is always better to think about such matters right from the outset, before the introduction of a new technology. That way data protection principles can be 'baked in' to those systems. Article 25 of the GDPR requires data protection by design and by default.

3.3 Refgrunt (librarians venting publicly about interactions with patrons)

One area in which librarians need to take particular care is over what is known as 'Refgrunt'. This refers to the genre of blogging/writing where librarians vent publicly about their interactions with patrons. The term 'refgrunt' can be traced back to a blog of that name which a librarian kept for about a year back in the early 2000s. The term 'refgrunt' could cover: blogs maintained by librarians; social media accounts maintained by librarians; and books written by librarians in which they describe their interactions with library users.

Sally Stern-Hamilton, writing under the pseudonym Ann Miketa, wrote a book entitled *The Library Diaries* (Miketa, 2012) about the demanding or atypical patrons she encountered at her library assistant job all day. From the introduction to the book: 'After working at a public library in a small, rural Midwestern town for fifteen years [which she calls Denialville], I have encountered strains and variations of crazy I didn't know existed in such significant portions of our population.'

The publisher's description said: 'Open this book and you'll meet the naked patron, the greedy, unenlightened patrons, destination hell, horny old men, Mr Three Hats, and a menagerie of other characters you never dreamt were housed at your public library.'

If a librarian were to write a book about their interactions with library patrons, that could potentially involve a number of privacy risks. If, for example, a librarian were to blog about the interactions that they had had with library users that day, and spoke about their frustrations regarding certain patrons, they would need to be particularly careful not to identify who they were referring to. This may not always be as straightforward as it might sound. Identification is not necessarily limited to situations where a person is named directly. It is possible that other information could lead to them being identified inadvertently.

If a librarian were to write a book about the users who frequented their library, would it be fair for some of those users to find out subsequently that by entering the library they had put themselves at risk of becoming a key character in a novel, where their mannerisms are described in such detail that they are easily identifiable?

3.3.1   The risk of being dooced

What people post on social networking sites raises privacy concerns. Indeed these can have severe consequences, such as someone being 'dooced' (that is, dismissed from their employment because of what they have written on a website or blog).

Many librarians maintain blogs, microblogs or social media accounts. Some of the large tech companies go out of their way to ensure that users can only have a single account, or that everything links back to one account. This poses a problem for anyone who wishes to make a clear distinction between their work life and their personal life. The organisation that they work for may well have a policy covering the use of social media. It may well include a clause to the effect that misuse of social media could result in disciplinary action up to and including dismissal.

3.4   Online databases and personalisation

Many online databases try to help users by providing a number of personalisation features. However, this involves a trade-off with user privacy. In order to personalise the service, to tailor it to their needs, the database inevitably needs to know the user's identity.

Utilising data such as what books a library user has read, what articles they have looked at, their click-behaviour, and what search terms they have used, it is possible on the plus side to provide them with a more tailored service. Algorithms can be deployed to anticipate what information that user would like to see based on their location, previous search history, etc.

Otherwise, they would get the generic, standard service. A lot of people are happy to give up some of their privacy in exchange for a more tailored service. And that is absolutely fine, provided that the user is making an informed choice.

Think of the online databases that your institution subscribes to. Do you or your users:

- create saved searches that you can run as required?
- create alerts so that users are automatically informed of new material matching their interests?
- make use of personalisation features such as a list of companies whose share price you monitor, or the industry sectors and sub-sectors that you monitor regularly?
- bookmark articles of interest?
- annotate items?

⟿Questions to consider when thinking about the privacy implications of personalisation

- Are library staff confident that the database vendor will keep this information secure? If so, what makes them so sure?
- Are data security commitments adequately covered in the contract?
- Does the library monitor the vendor on an ongoing basis, to see that they are living up to what was promised in the contract?
- Has the library user given informed consent to the use of personalisation?
- Is it possible for a user to opt out of the personalisation features?

Personalisation is a double-edged sword. There are undoubtedly many advantages to having a more tailored, more personalised service. However, there are also a number of downsides to personalisation. It means that companies can gather huge quantities of data about each individual. In a library context this begs a number of questions:

- Do library vendors 'own' that data?
- Do they share it with third parties?
- Do they delete the data once a user's account has been inactive for a defined period, such as one year?

3.4.1   The filter bubble

One downside of personalisation is the concept of echo chambers, or what Eli Pariser calls 'the filter bubble', where people become isolated within their own ideological bubbles and are continually served up with content that seems to be more of the type that they have looked at before. This ultimately skews their perception of the world. It allows less room for the chance encounters that bring insight and learning.

Pariser quotes Clive Thompson as saying that 'it's a civic virtue to be exposed to things that appear to be outside your interest', and that 'blind discovery is a necessary condition for scientific revolution. Because we have no idea what we're looking for.' Think, for example, of Einstein, Copernicus or Pasteur.

> There is no 'standard' Google anymore. Now it's a one-way mirror reflecting your own interests while algorithmic observers watch what you click, what you search for, what browser you use, where you log in from and so on. This does a disservice to serendipity. The company doesn't give people the chance to hit a 'dissonance' button if they want to hear a different viewpoint. Google is great at helping us find what we know we want, but not at finding what we know we don't want.
>
> (Pariser, 2012, 104)

Indeed, Rainee and Anderson (2017) point out that algorithms are aimed at optimising everything. They can save lives, make things easier and conquer chaos. Still, experts worry they can also put too much control in the hands of corporations and governments, perpetuate bias, create filter bubbles and cut choices, creativity and serendipity.

3.5   Telephone notification

Library services need to have a way of notifying users that the item(s) they have requested on hold have now arrived and are ready for them to collect. This is usually done by e-mail. However, there are some libraries who call their users when an item is ready for collection.

In one instance, a member of library staff called the user to inform them that the item they had requested was now ready for collection. The library user wasn't home at the time, and so a voice-mail was left. The message included details of the book title. What if that book had been about domestic violence? What if the message was picked up by the partner of the library user?

Where a library notifies a user by phone that the book/item they have requested is now available for collection, they should not give the details of that item over the telephone unless they can be absolutely sure that they are speaking with the user who requested the item. If the member of library staff has to leave a message, it is best simply to say that an item they have requested is now ready for collection from the library without specifying any further details.

3.6   Co-location

Co-location – the practice of placing several services in a single location – can take many different forms. It could, for example, cover the bringing together of council services such as a library, housing, tourism and customer service facilities.

The Libraries TaskForce blog has a case study of co-location in Stockton, where several different forms of co-location have been deployed: 'In Stockton, we already have experience of co-locating our libraries, with three sitting alongside customer service centres, one with a town council and two with Children's Centres. We were keen to look for other opportunities and a co-location with a community-focused mutual such as a Building Society fitted well with our strategy.' (Freeman, 2016).

There are undoubtedly a number of potential advantages where libraries are co-located with other services:

- It can lead to an increase in footfall.
- It can be more convenient when several council services are housed in the same building.
- The community hub model can have social benefits, leading to a greater sense of belonging to a community.

There are, however, a number of potential disadvantages. If it isn't well thought through, co-locating a number of services in a single location can threaten the level of privacy that library users are entitled to expect.

If a community hub or one-stop-shop approach is taken, how does this impact upon potential privacy and confidentiality concerns?:

- Does the co-location setup mean that potentially sensitive matters can be easily overheard (such as conversations relating to housing benefits or council tax)?
- Does the design of the enquiry booths provide sufficient privacy?
- Does the layout achieve the levels of privacy expected by the customer?

It is important to think through what can be done to minimise the risk to people's privacy, and whether those steps are necessary and proportionate. For example, Brighton's Jubilee library uses sound-masking technology to provide privacy and confidentiality for conference room users. The sound-masking emitters disrupt sound waves spilling out of the meeting rooms and into public areas, thereby improving the confidentiality of conversations (Lepore, 2017).

Maidenhead Council moved customer services from the town hall to the library. A library volunteer at Maidenhead library expressed concern at the lack of privacy in the library, as residents were forced to discuss private matters such as housing and benefits within earshot of library visitors (Witherden, 2017).

In the 2010s many police counters were closed, and indeed many police stations were shut down altogether, with the buildings being sold off. In the wake of those closures there have been a number of initiatives around the country involving members of the police being located in libraries as part of a 'one-stop-shop' approach (see, for example Strachan, 2016 and Express, 2016). Members of the public can then use an enquiry desk inside the library where they are able to speak to a uniformed member of police staff about crime reporting, general policing enquiries, road traffic collision reporting, applications for firearms licences, crime prevention advice and lost and found property.

Embedding members of the police inside libraries is seen by some as a controversial move. According to Clarke (2016a) 'police presence in libraries, no matter how abstract, normalises state surveillance'.

Another example of the potential risks involved with co-location is the acceptance that a selection of public libraries are becoming venues for processing UK visa information. It was announced in 2018 that the Society of Chief Librarians and UK Visas and Immigration (UKVI) had reached a deal in which UKVI kiosks were being set up in 56 public libraries in the UK:

> The new contract, delivered by IT consultancy Sopra Steria, will be rolled out across 56 library services in the UK and will enable visa applicants to submit biometric data and supporting documents. The role of library staff will be to support online access for applicants to submit their documents and biometric data, but they will not give visa or immigration advice, or know the results of visa applications.
>
> (Onwuemezi, 2018)

3.7   How long do you retain loan history data?

In order to be able to process personal data in accordance with the data protection principles, it is important to ensure:

- that the personal data is kept for no longer than necessary (the storage limitation in GDPR Article 5 (e) 'kept in a form which permits identification of data subjects for no longer than is necessary for the purposes for which the personal data is processed')
- that inaccurate data is erased or that the inaccuracy is rectified without delay (the accuracy principle in GDPR Article 5 (d), 'accurate and, where necessary, kept up to date; every reasonable step must be taken to ensure that personal data that are inaccurate, having regard to the purposes for which they are processed, are erased or rectified without delay').

Ask yourself: how long does your library retain loan history data? Is it: forever?;

for the default period used by your library management software provider?; or never (as soon as an item is returned, the record is anonymised or erased)? Do your users get a choice as to whether, and for how long, their reading history is retained?

3.7.1   E-book circulation data

Libby, by OverDrive, is an app for library e-books and audiobooks. The app shows a user's 'Activity', namely a list of the titles that they have borrowed, placed on hold, renewed and returned. Users have an element of control over the way their data is processed:

- Patrons are able to clear all titles from their Activity list, or remove a single title from the list
- Library users can turn off the Activity facility by tapping 'Disable Activity Recording'
- The software enables library users to clear their previous search history for audio and e-books.

3.7.2   Anonymising data so it is still available for statistical purposes

If the main reason for keeping data for more than a year is to be able to do a statistical analysis of circulation data, it is good practice to automatically anonymise the data at a fixed point in time.

By way of example, Newcastle libraries keep circulation history data for 12 months. After that, the data is anonymised, so that they still have information about the item having been borrowed but don't know by whom.

 TIP: Check that you have library software which incorporates the appropriate tools to anonymise library borrowing records, leaving it usable for statistical purposes. If that is not the case, make sure it is on your wish-list when you procure a new library management system.

3.8   Letting commercial interests into libraries

There are a number of examples of commercial companies providing digital literacy training. The types of companies that have offered training include Barclays Digital Eagles, Google Digital Garage and Lloyds Banking Group.

There are occasions where some companies have reached an agreement with the Society of Chief Librarians to offer such training. The training may be aimed at small businesses in the library's catchment area, or it may be aimed at individual library users.

In 2015, Lloyds Banking Group set an ambitious target of delivering 20,000 digital champions by 2017. Employees of the banking group were given training so that they could help people and organisations to improve their digital skills and financial capability. Halifax partnered with the Society of Chief Librarians, making it a corporate partner to offer digital champions to support IT taster sessions run in libraries across the UK.

Ayub Khan, a former President of CILIP, made the point that:

> Private sector partnerships are one way forward when public funding is in short supply. Libraries have worked with Barclays and the Halifax (digital volunteers) and BT (Wi-Fi). Google has set up Digital Garages aimed at businesses in larger libraries. Though ostensibly 'free', such initiatives are, at least in part, commercially driven. Libraries need to be aware, if not wary, of that.
>
> (Khan, 2016, 45)

•◆ Where commercial companies have been brought in to offer digital skills training, have the libraries involved sought any assurances regarding the privacy of their library users?

3.9   Use of CCTV in libraries

Randall and Newell (2014) undertook some research into the use of CCTV in libraries, and they looked specifically at the policies and practices of four large libraries which had installed video surveillance - three in the USA and one in the UK. They found that CCTV cameras had initially been installed either as a response to specific incidents of crime or as part of the design of new buildings.

> Libraries have long maintained strong protections for patron privacy and intellectual freedom. However, the increasing prevalence of sophisticated surveillance systems in public libraries potentially threatens these core library commitments.
>
> (Randall and Newell, 2014)

The CILIP guide to privacy in libraries suggests that people are too quick to consider CCTV as the solution to a problem without first thinking through whether there is an alternative: 'CCTV is . . . the first and apparently easiest solution available to management but, before its use, it should be clearly established that CCTV is a solution to the problem and that there are not other effective solutions with less impact on privacy' (CILIP, 2011, 14).

It is important to think through:

- Why do you want to install CCTV cameras in the library?
- Did you first consider whether there were any alternatives?
- If you install cameras, what safeguards will be built into your procedures to protect patron privacy?

Table 3.1 lists some of the considerations involved.

Table 3.1 *Things to consider before installing CCTV cameras*

Why do you want to install CCTV cameras?	Things to think through before installing CCTV cameras	What safeguards will there be in place to safeguard the rights of the individual?
To aid detection of crime	Have physical security measures been considered?	A written library CCTV code of practice or policy statement
To reduce crime, disorder and the fear of crime	Have risk assessments been performed?	CCTV viewing and recording equipment is only operated in accordance with the CCTV code of practice by trained and authorised users
To achieve a secure environment	Could the library's design layout be changed to make it easier to deter and detect problematic behaviour?	Signs to inform patrons that CCTV cameras are in use
To ensure the safety of staff and the public	Is it necessary and proportionate?	Access to the data captured by the cameras only available to the security team
To maintain the security of the library's assets (library resources and equipment)	Would dummy cameras deter potential disturbances or criminal behaviour?	The camera feeds are kept for a limited period of time
Preservation of the collection (e.g. in response to pages from rare books being removed and stolen)	Installation of mirrors in areas that are blind spots	Any covert or directed surveillance requires formal authorisation
Disturbances in the library	Are staff numbers sufficient to monitor everything?	

3.9.1   Why it is important to balance both privacy and security considerations

In order to respect the rights of individuals (their human rights, and specifically their right to privacy) it is important to ensure that there is a proper balance between the need to maintain personal privacy on the one hand and to achieve a certain level of security on the other.

The ALA's position in regard to video surveillance is:

> . . . high-resolution surveillance equipment is capable of recording patron reading and viewing habits in ways that are as revealing as the written circulation records libraries routinely protect. . . . Since any such personal information is sensitive and has the potential to be used inappropriately in the wrong hands, gathering surveillance data has serious implications for library management.
>
> (American Library Association, 2006)

Libraries should be transparent about their surveillance activities by posting signs and alerting patrons to the presence of the cameras, and should maintain written policies outlining the extent of video surveillance, policies related to retention and destruction of recorded footage, the potential uses of the video footage and the processes and procedures required prior to disclosure to third parties, including law enforcement.

3.9.2   Can libraries be too intrusive in their use of CCTV cameras?

Iowa City Public Library had security cameras in the library bathrooms. Susan Craig, the Public Library Director, said at the time that 'The reason the cameras are there is to protect people and to protect library property as well' (Collier, 2017).

Iowa lawmakers subsequently said yes to a bill banning cameras in restrooms and locker rooms at government buildings. The legislation applies to schools, libraries and other government buildings but has an exception for public hospitals. The legislation got through the Iowa Senate. It was approved without a single no vote. The cameras were subsequently removed from Iowa's public library bathrooms.

3.9.3   Cameras used to solve the disappearance of ancient books

Over a period of two years some 1,100 ancient books disappeared from a monastery's library without any trace of a break-in. It was only after the police eventually installed a hidden camera while the monks and nuns were attending Pentecost services that the mystery of how the books were disappearing was finally solved. As night fell, the police watched a man fill three suitcases with books. They arrested him while he was still carrying the rope he needed to scale the outer walls of the monastery. It ultimately led to the man being given a suspended sentence of 18 months for burglary (Webster, 2003).

The 12 guiding principles of the Surveillance Camera Code of Practice that system operators should adopt (Information Commissioner's Office, 2017a) are:

1   Use of a surveillance camera system must always be for a specified purpose which is in pursuit of a legitimate aim and necessary to meet an identified pressing need.
2   The use of a surveillance camera system must take into account its effect on individuals and their privacy, with regular reviews to ensure its use remains justified.
3   There must be as much transparency in the use of a surveillance camera system as possible, including a published contact point for access to information and complaints.
4   There must be clear responsibility and accountability for all surveillance camera system activities, including images and information collected, held and used.
5   Clear rules, policies and procedures must be in place before a surveillance camera system is used, and these must be communicated to all who need to comply with them.
6   No more images and information should be stored than that which is strictly required for the stated purpose of a surveillance camera system, and such images and information should be deleted once their purposes have been discharged.
7   Access to retained images and information should be restricted and there must be clearly defined rules on who can gain access and for what purpose such access is granted; the disclosure of images and information should only take place when it is necessary for such a purpose or for law enforcement purposes.
8   Surveillance camera system operators should consider any approved operational, technical and competency standards relevant to a system and its purpose and work to meet and maintain those standards.
9   Surveillance camera system images and information should be subject to appropriate security measures to safeguard against unauthorised access and use.
10   There should be effective review and audit mechanisms to ensure legal requirements, policies and standards are complied with in practice, and regular reports should be published.
11   When the use of a surveillance camera system is in pursuit of a legitimate

aim, and there is a pressing need for its use, it should then be used in the most effective way to support public safety and law enforcement with the aim of processing images and information of evidential value.

12   Any information used to support a surveillance camera system which compares against a reference database for matching purposes should be accurate and kept up to date.

3.10   Fingerprinting as a form of ID for use of library system

Thousands of school libraries throughout the UK have for many years been using biometric technology to manage the process for pupils to take out books. Children have their fingerprints scanned, and these are then used to authorise the borrowing of library books.

The biometric technology is not just being used in school libraries. It is also being used for other school activities, such as recording attendance or for access control on the school premises.

Biometric systems are intended to replace library cards and save time and money in managing the libraries. However, the use of electronic fingerprinting systems in this way to manage loans of library books has raised a number of privacy concerns.

The pressure group Privacy International expressed the view that the practice breached both the Data Protection Act and the human rights of the individual children concerned. In response, the Department for Education and Skills and the Information Commissioner said at the time that parents could not prevent schools from taking their children's fingerprints (Ballard, 2006).

The law has changed since then, though, with the implementation of the Protection of Freedoms Act 2012. Chapter 2 of the Act envisages parental consent before the processing of children's biometric information can be permitted. The law on using fingerprints in school libraries is now as follows:

- Schools need permission from parents before they can take pupils fingerprints or scan their faces
- Even if the parents agree, pupils are entitled to refuse to take part under the Protection of Freedoms Act 2012.

Where a child objects to the processing of their biometric data:

- a school must not process or continue to process the data
- the child must be provided with a reasonable alternative to the biometric system.

3.11   Use of 'enrichment' on the library catalogue

Enrichment services integrate seamlessly with a library's catalogue or discovery layer. The use of enrichment services can help to maximise the use of books and other media in the library's collection by acting as a showcase for the available resources. This type of service is used by libraries in order to provide a dynamic showcase for the library's collection. They can include images of book covers, summaries, reader reviews and reading levels.

Content embedded in websites is a huge source of privacy leakage in library services. Book cover images can be particularly problematic. Without meaning to, many libraries send data to Amazon about the books a user is searching for. Book cover images are almost always the culprit. What source do you use for book covers?

- Amazon
- Content Café
- Google Books
- LibraryThing
- OCLC
- Open Library Covers API
- ProQuest Syndetic Solutions.

Eric Hellman (2016) points out two indications of where a third-party cover image is a privacy problem: the provider sets tracking cookies on the hostname serving the content; or the provider collects personal information, for example as part of commerce. He says 'I've come to realise that part of the problem is that the issues are sometimes really complex and technical; people just don't believe that the web works the way it does, violating user privacy at every opportunity'.

Other commentators have also looked at the privacy issues involving book covers and social sharing and they believe that vendors are increasingly aware of this issue and that some of them proxy or cache images to avoid privacy problems.

3.12   Insecure software

Imagine a university library that uses a discovery service and citation software from the same supplier. Imagine, further, that whilst using the library's discovery software one of its patrons finds a reference that they think looks interesting and which they want to keep a note of. They therefore decide to export the reference to the citation software, but when they try to do so they are confronted with the kind of message shown in Figure 3.4 on the next page.

> ## Security warning
> The information you have entered in this page will be sent over an insecure connection and could be read by a third party
>
> Are you sure you want to send this information?
>
> ## CONTINUE   CANCEL

Figure 3.4 *Example of a security warning*

A couple of things to reflect on:

- Does the notice provide the library patron with sufficient information for them to be able to make an informed choice as to whether they wish to continue?
- Is it acceptable that a user is confronted with the stark choice of either using the service in a way that doesn't protect their privacy or else not bothering to use the service at all?

Given that both the discovery service and the citation software come from the same supplier, surely this is a good example of where the library should take the problem to the vendor to find out why the message comes up, and what can be done to rectify it.

3.13   Use of web analytics tools on library sites

Many libraries use web analytics tools on their websites, and a significant number of them use Google Analytics. But have they considered the privacy implications of doing so?

In the academic literature there is a case study of Cornell University Library, which has used Google Analytics (GA) to track website usage. However, given the tradition in libraries to protect reader privacy they felt that a compelling argument could be made that Google Analytics is inappropriate for libraries. As a result they selected Piwik (which is now known as Matomo, https://matomo.org) as a replacement for GA, on the basis that it was more respectful of user privacy. The case study explains why they selected Piwik, and describes what is involved when migrating from GA to Piwik (Chandler and Wallace, 2016).

Marshall Breeding undertook a survey of academic and research libraries (Breeding, 2016). Using the Ghostery plug-in for Chrome, he looked for all the tracking mechanisms that could be detected on the library website, online catalogue or discovery interface. The following list of tracking mechanisms were found to be present:

- Google Analytics
- Ajax search API
- Google AdSense
- Google Translate
- Google Tag Manager
- DoubleClick (owned by Google)
- Yahoo Analytics
- Adobe Omniture Analytics
- Adobe Tag Manager
- Adobe TypeKit
- Facebook Connect
- Facebook Social Plugin
- Twitter Button
- AdThis
- Piwik Analytics
- Crazy Egg
- WebTrends
- New Relic.

3.14   Use of cloud computing services to store personal data

Cloud computing solutions are being used by many public, academic and special libraries. They use the technology to meet their IT requirements in a way which balances cost effectiveness and flexibility whilst addressing user needs.

One example of library adoption of cloud computing is the New York Public Library. According to Gaudin (2016) the library moved its web infrastructure to the cloud, involving approximately 80 websites. They selected Amazon Web Services as their cloud provider. A big driver for moving to the cloud was the need for reliable websites.

The three primary cloud computing models are:

1 IaaS (infrastructure as a service) [example: Amazon web service]
2 PaaS (platform as a service) [example: Windows Azure]
3 SaaS (software as a service) [example: Google Apps].

Cloud computing embodies five characteristics (IT World, 2012):

1 on-demand self-service
2 rapid elasticity
3 broad network access
4 measured service
5 resource pooling.

Cloud systems can be public or private. The key privacy issues are:

- cloud services are typically provided by third parties
- whether the personal data gathered is protected through encryption or anonymisation
- whether the data is held outside the European Economic Area (EEA) in countries with less rigorous data protection laws
- meeting the requirements of the sixth data protection principle on data security
- who controls and owns the data.

3.14.1 Potential risks/threats
Control and ownership

- Barron and Preater, 2018, 94) note that cloud computing comes with a 'Faustian bargain' relieving systems librarians of the need to maintain servers, install updates, and deal with technical issues themselves but also shifting control over those systems to the supplier.
- In a cloud environment our data is no longer stored and processed on our computers. We therefore no longer control our data.
- Privacy is a major issue in the cloud because control of information stored and transmitted is never actually in the users' possession.

Reliance on third parties

Cloud computing involves the storage of often sensitive personal or commercial information in central database systems run by third parties. It therefore raises concerns about data privacy and security as well as the transmission of data across national boundaries (Carr, 2009).

Ability of cloud providers to make the data available to law enforcement agencies (and other third parties) without the client's knowledge

- Data can potentially be turned over to law enforcement agencies without the knowledge or consent of the client institution.
- Quoting Robert Gellman, Pariser says that the cops will love this (cloud computing). They can go to a single place and get everybody's documents (Pariser, 2012, 146)
- The very nature of cloud computing means that data may be stored on a variety of servers based in different locations across the world and may therefore be subject to access by various law enforcement or intelligence agencies under different legal regimes.
- Users are neither able to control the disclosure of personal data to third

parties nor to check if the software service providers have followed the agreed-upon privacy policy. Therefore, disclosure of the users' data to the software service providers of the cloud raises privacy risks (Wohlgemuth, Sonehara and Muller, 2010).

Zimmer (2015) notes that 'the use of cloud computing in libraries . . . has the potential to disrupt longstanding ethical norms within librarianship dedicated to protecting patron privacy'.

An example of the potential risks from use of cloud computing is where data on millions of Dow Jones customers was potentially exposed to unauthorised access on Amazon Cloud due to a configuration error (Chalfant, 2017).

3.14.2 Protections

There are a number of potential protections:

- **Encrypting the data:** 'any personally identifiable information and user data housed by the library offsite (cloudbased infrastructure, tape backups, etc.) should use encrypted storage' (American Library Association, 2015; 2016b).
- **Not giving personal data to the cloud provider:** the marketing material for bibliotheca.com's cloud library says that 'No private data is held on our systems about your users. All user-sensitive information is held within your LMS, not in our systems, allowing you to retain control of your library data and provide peace of mind to your users' (Bibliotheca, 2016).

3.15 Offshoring and outsourcing

Swartz (2004) says 'When companies offshore business processes, they are putting consumers' most sensitive personal information at risk – and there's little consumers can do about it'. Swartz was writing from the perspective of American companies, and her comments relate to the legislation in place in America at the time. She points out that offshoring poses risks to the security and privacy of consumers' personal data because when companies offshore business processes they also send their customers' most sensitive information overseas; and that many of the companies that contract for such work are based in countries which have far weaker security and privacy laws.

It is important to ensure that outsourcing contracts contain provisions allowing customers to claim for damages where suppliers breach their contractual agreement. Commercially it is also critical to ensure that there are 'back-to-back' warranties and indemnities to cover the data controller for any claims against it as a result of any failures of the processor.

⤙Outsourcing checklist

If you decide to use an external organisation to process data on your behalf, take steps and ask questions as follows.

- Carry out due diligence on the outsourcing provider (and be able to evidence this).
- Select a reputable organisation (are they the market leader or a small operator?).
- Check whether they are financially stable.
- Do they have a track record of similar assignments?
- Ask for the name and contact details of some supplier references.
- How willing are they to provide warranties and indemnities, and do these provide the protection you need?
- Do they indemnify you against regulatory fines?
- Ensure the organisation has appropriate physical and technical data security measures in place.
- Have you asked sufficiently probing questions regarding cybersecurity?
- Ensure the processor has robust staff vetting procedures in place, making appropriate security checks on staff.
- Ask to see staff training policies and monitoring records – e.g. can the third party confirm whether or not staff have completed data protection or cybersecurity training in the last 12–24 months and demonstrate it?
- Ensure that if you need to transfer personal data to a non-EEA processor, it is possible to do so in compliance with the GDPR.
- Ensure the written contract with the data processor is enforceable in the UK (and if located elsewhere, the jurisdiction of the processor).
- Require the processor to report any security breaches or any security problems.
- Require the processor to notify you of any requests for personal data from other jurisdictions.
- Can offshore activities be terminated immediately upon discovery of a significant breach?

Where IT services are outsourced to cloud providers, the data controller remains responsible for ensuring that processing complies with the DPA. So, even if you decide to use another organisation to process personal data for you, you remain legally responsible for the security of the data and for protecting the rights of the individuals whose data is being processed. It is essential to bear this in mind, because the reality is that cybersecurity breaches often involve failings by third-party IT providers.

Any potential appointment of a sub-processor by the data processor should always be caveated with the data controller having to approve any such appointment, as it will remain liable under the DPA for that processing and any breach. The due diligence it should perform on any data processor would also apply to any sub-processor.

Brown surveyed six law firms that had outsourced their law libraries, and found that:

> None of the law firms considered that outsourcing posed a greater risk to the security of confidential information. On the contrary, all six law firms believed that the outsourced service model strengthened the security of information because outsource service providers had introduced security procedures for the first time in place of the system of trust that had been relied upon to protect information within law firms previously.
>
> (Brown, 2014, 189)

3.16 Zines, libraries and privacy issues

(Fan)zines are usually devoted to specialised and often unconventional subject matter. They are often a vehicle for radical voices: they could be political, feminist, LGBT, and so on. They are ephemeral in nature, and often have very small print-runs. Initiatives to digitise fanzine collections pose a potential privacy threat. Not all zine makers want their names listed on the internet.

Digitisation of fanzines from many decades ago can throw up privacy issues – fans may have used their formal legal name (rather than a pseudonym), fully in the expectation of privacy, where the material was produced a long time before the world wide web was invented, and where the circulation of the fanzines was quite limited. Bussee and Hellekson (2012) say '. . . many fans published under their legal names, before the adoption of pseudonyms became commonplace. The full names of many fans thus appear in print on the cover of fanzines, in their tables of contents, and in ads circulated to market the zines. . . . These fans . . . deserve privacy.' The Zine Librarians Code of Ethics says that:

> Zine librarians/archivists should strive to make zines as discoverable as possible while also respecting the safety and privacy of their creators. . . . We should consult with zine creators and communities and respect the desires for autonomy and privacy of those creators and communities. We should not expose the legal identities of zine creators in cases where those identities are not explicitly noted in the zines themselves. We want zine makers to feel safe having their zines in our libraries.
>
> (Zine Libraries, 2015)

There's a need for searching and using the library with a degree of privacy and untraceability 'rather than give the government fodder to harass them' (Hedtke,

2007, 41). The idea of privacy and trackless searching and use is often a very important principle for infoshops. There's a risk that easy availability of information about zine makers, and those who are interested in their zines, could be used to flag people up to the authorities.

There are a number of examples of people talking of setting up separate public and private catalogues in order to keep certain information such as zine makers' names more private. Vermillion (2009) writes that 'we have been contacted to remove a last name from our database that was associated with a zine title that the author felt damaged her reputation in her current career – at age 16, she had no idea that the flippant title would ever be available online'.

3.17   Books on Prescription

The Reading Agency's Reading Well 'Books on Prescription' scheme is an example of bibliotherapy (the use of books in the treatment of mental or psychological disorders), where high-quality books are employed to achieve therapeutic effects. It helps people to manage their well-being using self-help reading. The scheme is endorsed by health professionals and supported by public libraries (Reading Agency et al., 2016).

Bibliotherapy schemes can now be found in libraries all over the world, involving public libraries, health/hospital libraries and academic libraries.

The recommended main reading list for the Books on Prescription scheme consists of books that provide evidence-based self-help for a variety of conditions (Table 3.2).

Table 3.2 *Topics covered by the Books on Prescription scheme*

Anger	Depression	Relationship problems
Anxiety	Health anxiety	Self-esteem
Binge eating/Bulimia	Obsessions and	Sleep problems
nervosa	compulsions	Social phobia
Chronic fatigue	Panic	Stress/worry
Chronic pain	Phobias	

There are a number of recommended reading lists:

- Reading Well common mental health conditions book list
- Reading Well Books on Prescription for dementia book list
- Reading Well for young people book list.

The idea is that healthcare professionals (including GPs), where appropriate, can prescribe self-help reading from approved lists of books available in public libraries to patients with mental health conditions which are collected from the local library. The scheme focuses on making self-help publications more readily available to patients suffering with a range of health problems.

Health data is one of the special categories of personal data that merits a higher level of protection (see Figure 1.1 on p. 4 – sensitive personal data). It should be processed in a manner which ensures appropriate security of that sensitive personal data. The sixth data protection principle relates to integrity and confidentiality and requires the use of appropriate technical or organisational measures. In other words, it isn't just a question of technological solutions.

3.18 Implications of GDPR for archiving information about living individuals

Many heritage institutions have digitised and catalogued print-based sources and are now gathering born-digital content on a large scale. This includes electronic personal archives and digital information in a variety of formats. This raises important legal and ethical issues, of which privacy is one. Public confidence and trust in data governance is crucial. Consequently, there are huge barriers to data sharing because of the data protection considerations.

Schedule 2 Part 6 Paragraph 28 of the DPA 2018 applies where personal data is processed for archiving purposes. The safeguards are that the data is processed in accordance with GDPR Article 89(1), as supplemented by section 19 of the DPA.

Article 89(1) says:

> Processing for archiving purposes in the public interest, scientific or historical research purposes or statistical purposes, shall be subject to appropriate safeguards, in accordance with this Regulation, for the rights and freedoms of the data subject. Those safeguards shall ensure that technical and organisational measures are in place in particular in order to ensure respect for the principle of data minimisation. Those measures may include pseudonymisation provided that those purposes can be fulfilled in that manner. Where those purposes can be fulfilled by further processing which does not permit or no longer permits the identification of data subjects, those purposes shall be fulfilled in that manner.

The regulation provides limited exemptions for organisations 'archiving in the public interest'. However, in order to enjoy these exemptions an organisation archiving in the public interest has a legal obligation to 'to acquire, preserve, appraise, arrange, describe, communicate, promote, disseminate and provide access to records of enduring value for general public interest' (GDPR recital 158).

Section 41(2) of the DPA 2018 sets out the situations where the processing would not satisfy the requirements of Article 89(1). It says that:

> The processing is not permitted if –
> (a) it is carried out for the purposes of, or in connection with, measures or decisions with respect to a particular data subject, or
> (b) it is likely to cause substantial damage or substantial distress to a data subject.

A survey conducted in spring 2017 focused on the process of decision making by digital librarians for take-down requests in digital collections at Association of Research Libraries (ARL) member institutions (Dressler and Kristof, 2018). Questions they considered include:

- Where does the issue of one's right to privacy and 'forgetting' stand with regard to openly accessible digital collections?
- Does an individual have a right to privacy within digital collections, or are freedom of expression rights more important?
- Do individuals deserve privacy and forgetting more than the public deserves an accurate and unabridged account of events?

Whereas the Google Spain case (C131/12) was centred on a take-down request by a private citizen to a major search engine of an old news item printed a decade before, the ARL survey focused on requests made directly to the institution publishing the digital content.

Institutions were asked if they had a policy, procedure or guidelines in place to address take-down requests of content on their website. Eleven institutions (40%) responded that they had a policy in place. Nine institutions (32%) responded that they did not have any kind of policy in place, and eight institutions (29%) reported that a draft to address this issue was in the works.

The ARL survey found that there was a lack of standard policies and practices; indeed, it highlighted enormous differences in how take-down requests are currently handled. The professional librarians surveyed displayed a broad array of personal opinion and thought processes revolving around take-down requests, and this is evident in the outcomes of such requests. Institutions may not wish or be able to conform fully to professional organisations' model policies or standards of practice once they are developed, but at the very least, discussions should take place across institutions and patrons should be provided with contact information.

3.19   Volunteer-run libraries

3.19.1   Building a relationship of trust with the user

Protecting the privacy of library users requires a genuine sense of trust on the part of the library user in library staff to respect their privacy. Michael Gorman emphasises the importance of trust with regard to issues of privacy and confidentiality:

> Our privacy codes need to be updated so that we can deal with modern circumstances without ever compromising our core commitment to privacy as an important part of the bond of trust between libraries and library users. That bond of trust is a precious thing and one that we should do our best to preserve. In the face of the onslaught of technology, it is more than ever important to preserve human values and human trust so that we can demonstrate that we are, above all, on the side of the library user and that user's right to live a private life.
>
> (Gorman, 2000, 156-7)

> In practical terms, much of the relationship between a library and its patrons is based on trust, and, in a free society, a library user should be secure in trusting us not to reveal and not to cause to be revealed which resources are being used and by whom.
>
> (Gorman, 2015, 185)

Many councils see volunteer-led libraries as sitting outside their statutory remit and offer them varying degrees of support, or none at all. Thinking from the perspective of the library user, would you put your trust in a fragmented and unregulated service to respect the privacy and confidentiality of your personally identifiable information?

Genuine concerns have been raised. For example, a library user in Derby is quoted as saying 'As regards data protection, I, for one, would not welcome an un-checked volunteer having access to my private details' (Hawley, 2017).

CILIP (2019) notes that 'For the first time volunteer figures are above 50,000, with the total of 51,394 up by 3,369 on 2016/17 figures' (referring to the CIPFA statistics). Where volunteers are involved in the delivery of library services, the question arises as to whether that bond of trust might be at risk in any way (and if so, what can be done to address that).

It would be totally wrong to suggest that volunteers somehow cannot be trusted to keep user information confidential, simply because they are volunteers. The root of the problem is that the way in which library services are being delivered is changing; is increasingly becoming more fragmented and more complex; and it is in this context that one has to ask whether library authorities are providing all volunteers with the training and support that they need.

A report by the Women's Institute (2013, 18) on the volunteer perspective in community managed libraries notes 'It is concerning that the lack of guidance available to community managed libraries regarding training and legal requirements leaves volunteers - at best - vulnerable and, at worst, potentially liable. This is not only worrying - both for the well-meaning volunteer and library user, but also unfair.'

It is clear that local authorities strapped for cash have looked to a variety of different ways in which they can reduce the money spent on libraries. These include closing branch libraries, reducing the library opening hours, reducing the number of professional librarians, reducing the number of paid staff, becoming more reliant on the use of volunteers, and moving some of their library branches over to a different business model such as community-managed libraries. In doing so they have had to wrestle with data protection and privacy considerations. For example, Derby City Council had to rethink their plans to hand over ten of the city's libraries into community ownership. Ultimately the council allocated further monies to address a number of issues, including ones around data protection:

> Some of the additional money will be used . . . to resolve the problem of volunteers being able to access data on the library computer systems independently of council library staff in order to remain compliant with the Data Protection Act. Council officers are looking into the possibility that library users may have to be contacted individually to give their consent for volunteers to access their data.
>
> (Hawley, 2018)

3.19.2 Volunteers and sensitive personal data

Where library services are being delivered by volunteers, and where a number of different models are being used, the fear is that not all of those volunteers will have had detailed training on data protection issues; they may not have been given the support of the local authority and may not be familiar with the official policies in place that are designed to protect users.

Wylie (2014) highlighted concerns over the idea of volunteers administrating the 'Books on Prescription' scheme which is aimed at patients with mental health conditions. If the person picking up an item lives next door or just down the street from the person issuing it, would you feel comfortable being served by a volunteer if you wanted to borrow a title such as *Overcoming Low Self-esteem*, *Break Free From OCD* or *Overcoming Binge Eating*, all of which are titles covered by the scheme?

3.19.3 Disclosure and Barring Service (DBS) checks (formerly CRB checks)

The need for library staff to undergo Disclosure and Barring Service (DBS) checks is considered obvious and essential to many people in cases where they have close, regular contact with children or with vulnerable adults, and/or where they have routine involvement with library users, often on deeply personal issues.

Volunteers may not need to be checked where they are doing jobs such as helping to re-shelve books or helping with back office work. But the number of volunteers has grown significantly in recent years. In some libraries there are no paid staff, and the library is run entirely by volunteers. Where they are the only presence in libraries, there is a strong case for them undergoing DBS checks (Lincolnshire Echo, 2012).

The way in which library services are being delivered has been undergoing a significant change in recent years. A number of different service delivery models can be found both within a library authority, and between different library authorities. A number of library services are using outside 'providers' such as pharmacies or community shops. The question arises as to whether councils should subject staff in these non-council local government offices to DBS checks, and if they don't, whether library users can be said to be able to expect the same level of privacy protection that they would from a paid member of library staff.

3.19.4 Data protection training

Are volunteers working in community-supported, community-managed and independent libraries provided with training on data protection and privacy issues, and if so, is the training adequate? Are volunteers up to date with IT, with health and safety procedures, confidentiality, data protection and so on?

Ensuring that all volunteers receive adequate training, and have a consistent level of knowledge across the entire library service, cannot be easy to achieve:

- Can you ensure that all volunteers are able to attend the training sessions that are offered?
- How often is the training delivered, given that volunteer turnover is likely to be greater than that of paid staff?
- The number of volunteers is much higher than full-time equivalent staff, so much so that local authorities have often found it necessary to create volunteer co-ordinator roles. The training would need to cover a lot of people, who may not all be available to attend a designated timeslot for training.

Wylie (2014) cites a 2011 blog post of the Friends of Gloucestershire Libraries which mentioned how library records contain information about people's addresses, details about vulnerable people - for example the housebound - and exemptions for foster children, fines and borrowing history and so on.

3.20 Copyright declaration forms

It is important that, at the point at which personal data is collected, data subjects are made aware of the ways in which their data will be used, and for them to be directed to the institution's privacy policy if they want further information about this. Doing so will ensure that the organisation is being open and transparent about their handling of personal data.

In the case of copyright declaration forms, the Libraries and Archives Copyright Alliance (LACA) has produced a set of model declaration forms, along with some accompanying guidance notes. These are available at http://uklaca.org/325. At the time of writing, these forms are in the process of being updated to reflect the requirements of the GDPR.

Libraries and archives that use copyright declaration forms need to communicate to the people whose personal data they are capturing in those forms precisely what they will or will not be doing with their personal data, and provide a link to the institution's privacy notice.

The purpose of the declaration form is to provide evidence in an infringement action that the librarian or archivist has acted lawfully. Once the requested copies have been supplied, the processing of the personal data is restricted to storage and use of that data in the event of copyright infringement proceedings. It is for this reason that the form must be preserved for six years plus the current year, in view of the Limitation Act 1980. It should be made clear to the data subject that the lawful basis for processing which applies in the case of copyright declaration forms does not permit the exercise of the right of erasure.

As an example, the National Library of Scotland uses a digital version of the copyright declaration form (https://shop.nls.uk/copy-enquiry-form). This makes clear that:

> Your personal information will be held and used by the National Library of Scotland for the purposes of responding to your enquiry and processing your order. For full information see our Privacy<www.nls.uk/privacy> page, in particular our Purchases<www.nls.uk/privacy/purchases-notice> and Enquiries<www.nls.uk/privacy/enquiries-notice> privacy notices.

CHAPTER 4

Case studies

4.1   Case study 1: CASSIE – Computer Access Software Solution

Librarica's CASSIE software (Computer Access Software Solution) contains features such as:

- access control and session timeouts
- print cost recovery
- reservations and waiting lists
- statistics reporting
- patron authentication through a live link to your circulation system
- visual management
- computer reservations through your library's website.

One feature that raises particular privacy concerns is the ability to view a patron's screen remotely. The feature is disabled by default, and can be enabled or disabled library-wide through the software's configuration settings. If the feature is enabled, it can be configured so that only selected staff members have access to that function.

The CASSIE software does allow libraries to display a customised usage policy statement that the user must accept at the beginning of each session before they are allowed access to the computer.

When asked whether there was any administrative function that permits the admin account to determine if employees have been using the remote viewing option, and if so, which employee, how often, and for which patron(s), Librarica's response was 'No. No record that a screen was viewed, whose screen was viewed, or screen image data, is logged or stored by CASSIE', and goes on to say that 'the system can be configured so that only selected staff members have access to the screen-viewing function' (Dissent, 2007).

At the time of the article by Dissent:

- If a user was looking at a particular website at a moment in time, and a librarian secretly accessed that user's screen remotely, no record was kept automatically of the screen (i.e. the web page) that the user was looking at –

which could have been something they didn't want others to know about, and could have been on an embarrassing, controversial or difficult topic.
• Where session statistics (computer name, session start time, session end time and session length) were enabled, they were kept for 30 days by default, but this could be overridden by an organisation-defined time period.

Helen Nissenbaum argues that privacy is best understood through a notion of 'contextual integrity', where it is not the sharing of information that is the problem, but the sharing of information outside socially agreed contextual boundaries. She proposes her 'framework of contextual integrity' (FCI) for analysis of potentially privacy-invading services and practices (Nissenbaum, 2010). The FCI consists of five key components:

1 contexts
2 informational norms
3 actors
4 attributes
5 transmission principles.

Nissenbaum asserts that the requirements of contextual integrity, which anchor privacy rules in social contexts and social roles, imply that laws applicable to the physical (bricks and mortar) world should apply to the online world.

The framework of contextual integrity can be used in order to analyse potentially privacy-invading services and practices. It is a useful tool that library services can make use of in order to anticipate potential problems when it comes to the introduction of new technologies or practices that may encroach on privacy. The framework provides a rigorous, substantive account of factors determining when people will perceive new information technologies and systems as representing a threat to privacy. It not only predicts how people will react to such systems but also formulates an approach to evaluating these systems and prescribes legitimate responses to them. Table 4.1 (pages 69–71) illustrates the application of the FCI to the CASSIE case.

If the new service or procedure generates changes in the actors, attributes or transmission principles, it is flagged up as violating entrenched informational norms and constitutes a *prima facie* violation of contextual integrity. CASSIE presents a potential conflict between patron's freedoms and autonomy, on the one hand, and institutional efficiency on the other (Nissenbaum, 2010, 183). Having said that, there are times where novel systems and practices can sometimes challenge traditional norms enough to justify changing them.

Table 4.1 *Application of the framework for contextual integrity to the CASSIE software*

Component	What the component covers	Application to the **CASSIE** case study
Contexts	Structured social settings with characteristics that have evolved over time. Contexts are characterised by • activities • roles, relationships, power structures • norms/rules (the duties, obligations, prerogatives, the privileges associated with particular roles, behaviours and whether they are acceptable or not) • internal values (goals, purposes and ends).	The delivery of library services has evolved and changed over time. For example, public libraries routinely use software for the purpose of content filtering – either through the blocking of specific sites or keyword blocking or a combination of the two. This is at odds with the professional and ethical duties of librarians towards their clients to provide uninhibited access to information and ideas. But the MAIPLE project (Cooke et al., 2014) found that users and librarians were both largely content with the use of such software. The CASSIE software violates existing privacy norms. Users would not normally expect a member of library staff to covertly access and remotely view their screen. Data gathered about their PC activity could potentially be shared with law enforcement agencies without the knowledge of the user whose data has been accessed. It could potentially happen in pursuit of investigations relating to national security, terrorism or criminal activity. Librarians have to know who borrows what specific items in order to be able to operate their service, otherwise they wouldn't be able to chase up overdue material, so that it is available for other users. However, software such as CASSIE expands the types of information that librarians have about their patrons to include details of what patrons are considering, exploring and looking up. As such CASSIE represents a *prima facie* violation of entrenched privacy norms.

Continued

Table 4.1 *Continued*

Component	What the component covers	Application to the CASSIE case study
Informational norms	These are concerned with the flow of personal information (transmission, communication, transfer, distribution and dissemination) from one party to another. Any breach of the context-relative informational norms is a key component in privacy breaches.	If there is no transparency about the types of data collected about them, and the reasons for collecting it, then established privacy norms are violated. The lack of any informed consent breaches the established norms. The CASSIE software does not warn a user when a member of library staff is actively looking at their screen. Even the admin account does not know whether or when staff members are using the remote access functionality. If a user was aware that their internet activity was being remotely monitored by library staff, or even if they just suspected that this was happening, it would have a chilling effect on their use, making them feel uncomfortable about the types of web pages they might look at, and be suspicious about what use might be made of that information or what conclusions anyone with that information might jump to.
Actors	• senders of information • recipients of information • information subjects 'It is relevant to know whether the actors are government or private, and in what capacity they act, among an innumerable number of possibilities' (Nissenbaum, 2010, 143).	Actors include: • library staff • library volunteers • library users • the software vendor • law enforcement agencies.

Continued

Table 4.1 *Continued*

Component	What the component covers	Application to the CASSIE case study
Attributes (information types, data field)	Are the attributes appropriate to the context? For example, who should have access to borrowing histories? Who should access someone's searching and browsing histories?	Accessing the details of websites a library user visits could qualify as processing of sensitive personal data. It could lead someone to jump to conclusions about an individual's political views, health condition or sexuality. Having data about websites visited without a complete picture as to the reasons why they were looking at those sites could lead to them creating an inaccurate or highly misleading profile of the library user. Just because someone looks at a website about Parkinson's disease does not automatically mean that they have the condition. They could, for example, be studying medicine or researching the condition because one of their friends has been diagnosed with the condition.
Transmission principles	This component expresses the terms and conditions under which transfers ought or ought not to take place. Transmission principles can act as 'a constraint on the flow (distribution, dissemination, transmission) of information from party to party in a context' (Nissenbaum, 2010, 145).	Accessing a user's screen remotely without telling the user that this would take place, and doing so covertly, cannot be justified as a matter of routine. Covert surveillance should only ever be considered if there is good reason to believe that a crime is taking place, and that there is no other way of gathering the necessary evidence. In such circumstances covert surveillance should only be undertaken for a limited period of time, not as a matter of routine. It should require authorisation at a senior level. Directed surveillance of that kind should only be undertaken for the purposes of a specific investigation. Its use should be justified and the reasons for using it should be recorded.

4.2   Case study 2: Library participation in learner analytics programmes

Learning analytics is the measurement, collection, analysis and reporting of data about learners, and the use of this data to improve learning and teaching.

There are growing pressures on libraries to integrate their data with institution-level data in learning analytics systems. A key driver is the perceived need to demonstrate a direct relationship between student interaction with the library and this having a positive impact on learning outcomes. It has led a number of libraries to begin feeding the data they collect into learning analytics systems so as to show that the way in which they deploy their resources and expenditures is in alignment with wider institutional goals (such as improving student success rates, being more efficient, cutting costs, etc.)

Some people have argued that the use of learning management systems has gone too far. For example, Jones and Salo (2018) point out that 'Oral Roberts University now pressures its incoming classes to purchase Fitbits, arguing that measuring student movement is part and parcel of fulfilling the institution's mission of educating the mind as well as the body and spirit. Step and heart-rate data from the Fitbits are automatically sent to the system and graded, but grades are lowered if they opt out.'

4.2.1   The data that can be captured and fed into a learning management system

The data that is fed into learning management systems consists of both static and fluid data.

Static data covers the data that is collected, recorded and stored by institutions such as student records, staff data, financial data or property/estates data. This can then be combined with **fluid data**, which refers to the types of data generated as a result of the increasingly digital way in which students interact with their university.

At the institutional level, examples of fluid data include swipe card data from access-controlled campus buildings and log-ins to the virtual learning environment (VLE). Fluid data on student interaction with the library include: e-book and journal article downloads; bookings onto library training sessions; circulation records; interlibrary loan records; and suggestions for new addition(s) to library. Table 4.2 shows the range of possible interactions.

Table 4.2 *How do library users interact with the library?*

What they use	What they attend	What they participate in	What they borrow
Journal article	Library facility	Training session	Book
E-book	Makerspace	Event (such as when a publisher comes to the library)	Interlibrary loan
Institutional repository	Study space with a technobooth	Group study session	Equipment (such as an i-Pad)
Library computer	Silent computer room		
Library printer	Assistive Technology Centre		

4.2.2   What protections are there in place to protect user privacy?

Rubel and Jones (2014) say that 'while the literature on learning analytics recognises potential privacy conflicts, there is little systematic discussion of the ways in which privacy and learning analytics conflict'.

Where an institution decides that data about a student's interactions with the library should be fed into the learning analytics system, the question that needs to be asked is what protections are there in place – or should be put in place – to protect the privacy of library users.

Examples of the practical steps libraries can take to protect user privacy include:

- anonymising the data by either removing or modifying information that could be used to identify a library user
- storing a truncated version of the classmark, so that the general subject category is given but it isn't possible to see the specific book title borrowed
- recording the library user's age at the time the transaction took place, rather than showing their precise date of birth.

Another example would be to have added protections in place for the most privacy-intrusive data. The Open University policy on the ethical use of student data for learning analytics states that:

> . . . sensitive information on religious belief and sexual life will not be used as part of the analytical models. Should any other sensitive data items be required for learning analytics, consent will have to be obtained

by a suitable means, such as through changes to the Data Protection Policy. Any combinations of data or derived data that may contravene an individual's right to respect for their private and family life will not be used.

(Open University, 2014)

Systematic data mining – especially of student behaviours and interactions with library resources – raises student privacy and intellectual freedom issues. Additionally, there are also practical questions regarding whether libraries have data management plans that carefully consider data anonymisation, de-identification, retention and deletion (Briney, 2018).

Rubel and Jones (2014) argue that proponents of learning analytics must address four narrow problems related to the use of student data:

1 Learning analytics systems should provide controls for differential access to private student data.
2 Institutions must be able to justify their data collection using specific criteria.
3 A full account is required of how the benefits of learning analytics are distributed between institutions and students.
4 Students should be made aware of the collection and use of their data and provide them with reasonable choices regarding collection and use of that data (are people allowed to opt out, or is there a stark choice between not giving consent or not enrolling?).

➥Learning analytics checklist
- Be transparent about why learning analytics is being used.
- Make data collection practices visible.
- Highlight the privacy-protecting activities you have in place.
- Ensure you have informed consent when you collect and use data.

4.2.3   Learning analytics and professional ethics
Jones and Salo consider how data mining practices run counter to ethical principles in the American Library Association's Code of Ethics. They address how learning analytics implicates professional commitments to: promote intellectual freedom; protect patron privacy and confidentiality; and balance intellectual property interests between library users, their institution, and content creators and vendors. They recommend that librarians should embed their ethical positions in technological designs, practices and governance mechanisms.

There is a real risk that as learning analytics matures, the ethical commitments that librarians have – not least with regard to privacy and confidentiality issues – will come under threat by institutional stakeholders who do not have the same professional values.

> We recommend that librarians advocate for their ethical positions within and outside the boundaries of their institution, participate in data governance practices to embed their values in information flows, and work closely with policy-makers to design policies in ways that consider their professional ethics.
>
> (Jones and Salo, 2018)

4.3   Case studies 3–6: Rollouts of a shared library management system

There have been a number of initiatives in recent years relating to shared digital services, such as having a shared library management system and/or a shared discovery system. These initiatives have included the sharing of systems across multiple institutions; or even across entire countries. Where personal data is being processed on a shared library system, the potential damage that can be caused if a data breach takes place increases exponentially not least because of the much higher number of library users than would be involved with a single institution.

4.3.1   Case study 3: WHELF shared LMS project

The Wales Higher Education Libraries Forum (WHELF) shared library management system (LMS) project consists of 11 institutions spread across nearly 90 library locations, has around 600 library staff, 170,000 customers and approximately 10 million bibliographic records.

The opportunities identified for the project include:

- single search across library collections throughout Wales
- reciprocal borrowing arrangements
- shared management information
- real-time analytics leading to improved service delivery.

Data protection and privacy considerations taken into account when tendering included:

- full compliance with the Data Protection Act
- use of cookies in compliance with the PECR

- managing access rights (for example, ensuring library staff can see only user records relating to their own institution)
- implementing security elements on the technology side (for example, encrypting SIP2 transmissions between local PCs and the servers)
- privacy impact assessment for the shared project.

4.3.2 Case study 4: Single digital presence for public libraries in England

The Sieghart Review (Sieghart, 2014) called for the feasibility of a single digital presence to be investigated. This recommendation was then passed on to the Libraries Task Force. As part of this process BiblioCommons (2016) wrote a report for the Society of Chief Librarians (now called Libraries Connected) which looked at how users experience their libraries currently and outlined an approach to building a single digital presence for public libraries.

Demand for a single digital presence in UK public libraries, and the possible shape this could take, are being explored by the British Library. The 18-month scoping project, funded by Arts Council England and the Carnegie UK Trust, will investigate user expectations and demand for what a national online platform for public libraries might deliver, and will explore the network of stakeholder groups and organisations best placed to make it a reality.

Exploratory studies into the feasibility of a single digital presence have identified a number of privacy considerations:

- the need for a careful balance between privacy and comprehensive data collection
- concerns about privacy and data sharing
- privacy settings and other safeguards at the individual and the aggregate level.

4.3.3 Case study 5: Single library management system for all public libraries in Ireland

The Irish Data Protection Commissioner (DPC) had an engagement with the Libraries Development Unit in the Local Government Management Agency (LGMA) in 2015 regarding the rollout of a single library management system (Sierra) for all public libraries in Ireland.

During the course of this engagement, the DPC flagged up a number of potential issues:

- issues surrounding consent
- issues relating to inappropriate access

- the need for access controls and trigger mechanisms
- the need for there to be built-in audit trail functionality (both read and edit access) in the finalised version of the Sierra system.

At the time of this engagement, the DPC singled out the Sierra library management project for future examination via an audit once the system went live across the majority of libraries in Ireland. Malahide Library was subsequently selected for audit.

Shortly before the August 2017 audit of Malahide library, Fingal County Council contacted the DPC informing them of a recent incident where a library staff member based in another local authority inadvertently came across the borrower record of a library borrower in Fingal containing data entries of a highly inappropriate, sexually explicit nature. Fingal County Council established subsequently that the records of 20 Fingal Library borrowers had been edited in this manner and these records had in fact been imported from the previous library management system, Galaxy, onto Sierra.

The DPC established that there was no audit trail functionality in relation to the amendment of borrower records on either the Galaxy or Sierra systems that would assist in identifying the source of the edits. It was further noted that library staff log in to Sierra with generic log-ins for each library. The Irish Data Protection Commissioner instructed the Libraries Development Unit in the Local Government Management Agency to take the following measures:

- Audit trail functionality should be implemented as a matter of priority, facilitating the generation of logs for all look-ups and edits on Sierra.
- Individual unique log-in usernames and passwords should be assigned to every individual user accessing the Sierra National Library Management system.
- Functionality should be built into Sierra whereby staff are automatically prompted to change their passwords on a regular basis.

The GDPR imposes a legal requirement on all data controllers to notify the DPC of a breach. Article 4(12) of the GDPR defines a personal data breach as a 'breach of security leading to the accidental or unlawful destruction, loss, alteration, unauthorised disclosure of, or access to, personal data transmitted, stored or otherwise processed'. Under the GDPR both the unauthorised access to and the alteration of borrower records in the manner outlined would constitute a notifiable data breach.

(This case study is based on information from the annual report of the Data Protection Commissioner (Ireland), 2017.)

4.3.4   Case study 6: Introduction of National Entitlement Cards in Scotland

In December 2008 Dr Geraint Bevan of NO2ID[1] (12/2008) made a freedom of information request:[2]

> On 13 November 2008, Ian Brown of Education and Lifelong Learning (Scottish Borders Council), wrote to library users about the introduction of a new Library Management System 'Vubis Smart'. The letter states that all users will be re-registered and that old library cards are to be replaced by National Entitlement Cards. No option is provided for library users to opt out of registering for such a card. . . . Please tell me:
>
> - whether any legal advice was taken before deciding to implement this system;
> - whether a privacy impact assessment has been conducted; and
> - whether the Information Commissioner's Office was consulted.

The response was:

> In terms of your specific requests
> The upgrading of the Information System and the updating of customer records are part of business as usual and therefore:
>
> - no legal advice was taken in relation to changing to the new Library Management System (Vubis Smart) or to require borrowers to re register,
> - a privacy impact assessment was not conducted,
> - the Information Commissioner's office was not consulted.

The requirement under the GDPR and the Data Protection Act 2018 for data controllers to undertake a data protection impact assessment where processing operations are likely to result in a high risk to the rights and freedoms of natural person relates not only to cases where new services are being introduced, but also to ones where changes are being made to existing services or procedures. The need for a DPIA cannot, therefore, be ruled out simply on the basis of claiming that it is 'business as usual' where an information system is being upgraded.

It is over a decade since the above FOI request was made, and since then we have seen the introduction of new data protection laws in the UK. The GDPR makes clear that what matters is not so much a question of whether we are talking about a new system or a change to an existing one, but rather whether it is likely to result in a high risk to the rights and freedoms of individuals (for more information about Data Protection Impact Assessments see Chapter 10).

Notes

1   NO2ID is public campaign group, formed in 2004 to campaign against the UK government's plans to introduce UK ID cards and the associated National Identity Register.
2   www.whatdotheyknow.com/request/privacy_assessment_of_library_ma.

CHAPTER 5

Cybersecurity

Cybersecurity has been defined as the protection of internet-connected systems, including hardware, software and data, from cyberattacks; or the practice of defending computers, servers, mobile devices, electronic systems, networks and data from malicious attacks.

As the old saying goes: 'Prevention is better than cure'. While Chapter 6 looks at breaches of personal data, this chapter considers steps that can be taken to reduce the risks of data breaches occurring in the first place and to limit any potential damage should such a breach take place.

According to the National Audit Office:

> . . . the internet is inherently insecure, and attempts to exploit its weaknesses – known as cyber-attacks – continue to increase and evolve. The risk of deliberate or accidental cyber incidents is heightened by the increasingly interconnected nature of networks, systems and devices in use by organisations and individuals. Government's view is that cyber risks can never be eliminated but can be managed to the extent that the opportunities provided by digital technology, such as reducing costs and improving services, outweigh the disadvantages.
>
> (National Audit Office and Cabinet Office, 2019)

The National Cyber Security Centre (2016) lists ten steps to cybersecurity:

1 set up your risk management regime
2 network security
3 user education and awareness
4 malware prevention
5 removable media controls
6 secure configuration
7 managing user privileges
8 incident management
9 monitoring
10 home and mobile working.

BigBrotherWatch (2018, 3) released a report based on freedom of information requests in which they found that the estimated number of cyberattacks experienced by local authorities – which hold the data of millions of residents – was 98 million between 2013 and 2017, which equates to 37 attacks every minute.

How robust is your IT security framework? Are you protecting your data, rather than just the perimeter around it? Do you have a complete picture of the personal data you process (see Chapter 9 on audits)? Are you spending sufficient time and money on cybersecurity? An ICO report from 2014 on learning from the mistakes of others identifies the top eight computer security vulnerabilities (Information Commissioner's Office, 2014b):

1   a failure to keep software security up to date
2   a lack of protection from SQL injection (a code injection technique, used to attack data-driven applications, in which malicious SQL statements are inserted into an entry field for execution by hackers)
3   the use of unnecessary services
4   poor decommissioning of old software and services
5   the insecure storage of passwords
6   failure to encrypt online communications
7   poorly designed networks processing data in inappropriate areas
8   the continued use of default credentials, including passwords.

The digital threat landscape is constantly changing. It is difficult to know the probability of any given attack succeeding, or how big the potential losses might be. No cybersecurity system can ever be said to be impenetrable. Cybersecurity isn't like that. It would be wrong to think of it as a finite problem that can be solved with a specific set of actions, as if you can claim to be secure as long as you are able to tick a series of boxes against a list of security measures. Rather, it is an ongoing process. It is more appropriate to think of it as a question of risk management.

⇢ Cybersecurity checklist

- Do you have policies covering access to your information systems, applications and data?
- Do you require library staff to change their passwords regularly?
- Are employees regularly reminded not to share their passwords with anyone else, and to keep them secure?
- Are sensitive files encrypted?
- Is there a policy on how long data should be held for?
- What measures are in place to protect payment card information?

- Can deleted data be recreated from log files, backups, caches, proxies and mirrors?
- Are there measures in place to prevent unauthorised BYOD devices from accessing sensitive business or personal information?
- Where BYOD devices are lost or stolen, is there a procedure in place to promptly revoke access to institutional information and services.

5.1　Least-privilege model

Do library staff have far wider access to sensitive information than is necessary for their job function? Do third parties have access to more information than is required for the role or function they perform? Do staff have the rights to edit records, when read-only access would be sufficient for their needs? The solution is to enforce a strict *least-privilege model* where insiders have access to data on a need-to-know basis. The least-privilege model refers to where you give minimal user profile privileges on computers, based on each user's job necessities. In other words, don't give anyone more user privileges than are absolutely necessary for them to perform their role.

All processes related to the identification and monitoring of employees who are at high risk of becoming malicious insiders - such as employees close to a termination or resignation date - need to be reviewed as part of an insider threat and vulnerability analysis.

It is important to pay close attention to who has access to the IT system. Imagine the following scenario:

The institution decides to update its computer system. It employs an IT contractor to do the work. Access to the IT system is set up for the contractor to be able to work from home. The institution subsequently has a dispute with the contractor over the quality of the work that has been done, and withholds payment until matters are resolved. In the meantime the contractor still has access to the system and uses it to delete all of the files on the institution's server. It is a criminal offence under section 3 of the Computer Misuse Act 1990 to carry out an unauthorised modification of material held on computer, when your intention is to prevent or hinder access to the data or impair its operational reliability. The offence is punishable by a fine or imprisonment, or both.

It may seem self-evident, but:

- Be careful about who can access the computer system.
- Be particularly careful about who has remote access to the computer system.
- Be prompt at disabling access for contractors and for employees as soon as they cease working for you.

- Take care with regard to members of staff who are serving out their notice period.

Gangadharan (2017) considers the IT issues that shape the conditions for library user privacy. She raises a number of questions that library managers need to consider. For example: is the library Wi-Fi password protected, or open for all to join? What kinds of security protocols does the library implement on its digital properties (e.g. mobile apps, website)?

↬Cybersecurity tips

- Identify your role – are you a data controller or a data processor?
- Ensure it is clear who has responsibility for dealing with cyber- and data security.
- Conduct risk assessments where appropriate and then act on the results.
- Ensure you have up-to-date security systems such as firewalls, encryption and authentication.
- Develop a cybersecurity policy – check regularly that it is being complied with.
- Ensure employees receive training on the cybersecurity policy.
- Make sure staff know when and how to report incidents internally.
- Test your cyber- and data security systems regularly (including penetration testing).
- Adopt a least-privilege model, where you restrict access to personal data to those in the library service who need to have access to it.
- Develop a detailed data breach response plan (see section 6.1 in the next chapter).
- Consider making financial provision to insure risks and to handle any data breaches.
- Keep records of any data breaches:
  - what data was compromised
  - how was the breach dealt with
  - what steps were taken to ensure that type of breach does not recur.
- Make use of the government's Cyber Essentials scheme and guidance on cybersecurity available from the National Cyber Security Centre.

West (2016) identifies two main ways in which libraries could be doing a lot better in the realm of cybersecurity:

1 advocating for patron privacy (library leadership should be advocating for cybersecurity more effectively)

2 providing information about existing threat environments (what do the threats look like and who really poses a danger to us?).

⟶Useful resources

The Cyber Essentials scheme is the government-backed, industry-supported scheme to help organisations protect themselves against common online threats: www.gov.uk/government/publications/cyber-essentials-scheme-overview.

National Cyber Security Centre guidance https://ncsc.gov.uk/information.

5.2　Offering training on cybersecurity and related topics

Libraries can play an important part in raising awareness of privacy, data security and online safety issues by hosting, co-ordinating or running training courses on topics such as:

- staying safe online
- your online safety, security and privacy
- protecting your privacy on the internet
- information security
- privacy and surveillance
- hosting a cryptoparty (see Glossary, p. 195).

Think about the training needs of library staff, volunteers, library users and local businesses.

Under the heading 'Ideas for your library' Scottish PEN (2018) suggests 'Develop bespoke training for local businesses with a focus on cyber-security and protecting data against third parties'.

In the USA the Library Freedom Institute (LFI), https://libraryfreedomproject.org/lfi, was a privacy-focused programme for librarians to teach them the skills necessary to thrive as privacy advocates, from educating community members to installing privacy software, and also to influencing public policy.

The Digital Privacy and Data Literacy Project (www.dataprivacyproject.org) teaches New York City library staff how information travels and is shared online, what risks users commonly encounter online, and how libraries can better protect patron privacy. The project is funded by the Institute of Museum and Library Services. Its training helps support libraries' increasing role in empowering their communities in a digital world. They have a curriculum page on their website (https://dataprivacyproject.org/curriculum) aimed at library and information professionals so that they can provide privacy training for their users. The curriculum contains a facilitator's guide, presentation slides and handouts, and permits remix and re-use under a Share Alike 4.0 Creative Commons Licence.

5.3   Protecting personal data

There are a number of tools which can be used to protect personal data so that it is impossible to identify specific library users or access the data about their use of library services:

- **Encryption** - the process of using an algorithm to transform data in order to make it unreadable for unauthorised users.
- **Hashing** - A hashing algorithm converts passwords of any length into a random, fixed-length string of characters.
- **Salt and pepper** - The salt is a mathematical tool that attaches more random characters to the hashed version of the password, normally at the beginning. Pepper attaches the random characters to the end of the hashed version. Together they make the hash even harder to crack and turn back into your password.

⇢ E-mail hacking tip

Enter your e-mail address into the website haveibeenpwned.com to find out whether your account is amongst those that have been hacked. The haveibeenpwned.com website is a database of stolen user accounts which is dedicated to informing victims. If your e-mail address has been compromised, change your log-in details as soon as possible.

5.4   Bring your own device (BYOD)

With the rapid increase in the use of mobile devices and the growth of remote and flexible working, staff now expect to use their own laptops, phones and tablets to conduct business.

Employees are also consumers in their own right. Many mobile devices are smart devices. People don't want to have to lug around two separate devices (one for work and one for personal use) if there is no need to do so.

But BYOD raises a number of data protection concerns, because the device is owned by the user rather than the data controller, while data controllers are required to ensure that all processing of personal data under their control remains compliant with the Data Protection Act 2018.

By considering the risks to data protection at the outset, a data controller has the opportunity to embed data protection at the core of its business activities and to raise overall standards.

An important question to consider is which personal data can be processed on a personal device (such as a laptop, phone or tablet owned by a member of library staff), either inside or outside the office.

The Data Protection Act 2018 requires employees to take measures against unauthorised or unlawful processing of personal data.

The Employment Practices Code states that employees are entitled to a degree of privacy in the work environment.

5.4.1 Plan for security incidents where devices are lost, stolen or compromised

Personally owned devices are routinely lost, stolen or compromised. Should one of these events take place, it is important to have confidence that any personal data stored on them is protected.

Plan for and rehearse security incidents. When an incident occurs you should:

- act immediately to limit losses
- revoke access to institutional information and services quickly
- prevent the spread of any compromise
- learn lessons from the incident.

Consider using a remote wipe feature for sensitive data to be removed from a personally owned device if it is lost or stolen, or if the staff member leaves the organisation. This will need to be reflected in the organisation's BYOD policy.

It is important to be transparent with members of staff, so that they are aware of the circumstances under which a device may be wiped and what that will actually do to their device (putting it back to its factory settings) and that the reason for the policy is to protect confidential or sensitive information that may be at risk. If they know this, they may actually prefer to have two separate devices.

5.4.2 Network architecture design

The security architecture is one component of a product's overall architecture and design and within that BYOD security can be incorporated into your network architecture. In addition, security needs to be built into policies and procedures. For example:

- Prevent unauthorised devices from accessing sensitive business or personal information.

- Ensure authorised devices can only access the data and services you are willing to share with BYOD staff.
- Clarify the responsibilities of the institution and those of staff members.
- Set out these requirements in an institutional BYOD policy.
- Ask staff to confirm their acceptance of the policy, and that they understand their obligations.
- Deploy 'defensive network architectures' to ensure access to business systems from personal devices is brokered via a service mediation layer (which restricts access to only the services permitted to be accessed by BYOD staff).
- Use protective monitoring solutions to try and detect attacks from compromised devices.

Devices may be infected with malware. Steps need to be taken to reduce the risk of the corporate network being compromised by end-user devices and unmanaged devices.

5.4.3   Network separation

To prevent devices from accessing data they are not permitted to, network separation should be used within the organisation's networks. [Use technical controls to] 'prevent users from accessing data they are not permitted to access from personally owned devices' (Out-law.com, 2014).

Where possible, technical controls should be used to prevent users from accessing data they are not permitted to access from personally owned devices. Services holding data not intended for consumption by personally owned devices should not be reachable from those devices where only a subset of data is required on the device, or read-only access is required. The policies should be enforced through the use of a reverse proxy to filter requests.

User accounts in use by BYOD staff should be distinct from accounts used on institutionally owned devices; passcodes must not be shared between accounts.

Conceptually, any solution built to provide access to internal services from personally owned devices should perform these four steps:

1 A secure tunnel provided by the device operating system or BYOD product terminates the encrypted session between the personally owned device and the corporate network boundary.
2 The user is authenticated to the corporate network, allowing the subsequent layers to provide access to only the data which that user is permitted to view on their device.
3 Access to internal services is brokered through a service mediation layer, such as a reverse proxy. These restrict access to only services permitted to

be accessed from personally owned devices, and may in addition filter those requests (for example, to make them read only).
4 Within the core network, services are logically separated to ensure that only specifically whitelisted (or pre-approved lists of) services which do not contain sensitive data are exposed. The organisation needs to consider what internal applications will be made available to BYOD staff, as this will not always be the same as for institutionally owned devices.

5.4.4   BYOD policies

The ICO's guidance (Information Commissioner's Office, 2016, 6-9, 11) outlines some of the key issues organisations need to be aware of when allowing staff to use personal devices for work:

- Be clear about which types of personal data may be processed on personal devices and which may not.
- Use a strong password to secure your devices.
- Use encryption to store data on the device securely.
- Ensure that access to the device is locked or data automatically deleted if an incorrect password is input too many times.
- Ensure that the device automatically locks if inactive for a period of time.
- Make sure users know exactly which data might be automatically or remotely deleted and under which circumstances.
- Maintain a clear separation between the personal data processed on behalf of the data controller and that processed for the device owner's own purposes, for example, by using different apps for business and personal use.
- Register devices with a remote locate-and-wipe facility to maintain confidentiality of the data in the event of a loss or theft.
- Make sure you have a process in place for quickly and effectively revoking access in the event of a reported loss or theft.
- Limit the choice of devices to those which you have assessed as providing an appropriate level of security for the personal data being processed.
- Provide guidance to users about the risks to downloading untrusted or unverified apps.
- Do not use public cloud-based sharing and public backup services which you have not fully assessed.
- Take care that monitoring technology remains proportionate and not excessive, especially during periods of personal use.

5.4.5   Ensure the BYOD policy is workable

It is important to balance technical controls with usability. Bad policies which are too restrictive and impact negatively on the usability of the device will drive down adoption, because staff won't follow the institution's official procedures and will instead explore possible workarounds, thereby undermining your policies and increasing security risks. This phenomenon is known as 'shadow IT', where staff want easier ways to be able to do their jobs.

Conduct regular audits of work-related data stored on devices. When staff leave the organisation or replace their device, ensure all work-related data is removed and access to institutional systems is revoked.

Staff should be made to authenticate themselves before being given access to work-related data. Since personally owned devices are more likely to be infected by malware, authentication credentials could be compromised. As a result, there should be a different set of credentials for BYOD access to institutional systems to those used for accessing the organisation's desktop environment. This is a list of questions to ask:

- When did you last undertake a security update?
- Do you regularly keep your software up to date?
- How good are your backups?
- What data loss detection controls do you have in place? These should be tested regularly to ensure that they will detect data leakage, and monitor the transfer of sensitive information outside of the organisation's network.
- Do the controls in place adhere to current security standards?

Kim (2016, 442) points out that institutions can protect their systems against vulnerabilities and intrusion attempts using systematic measures such as two-factor authentication, stringent password requirements and locking accounts after a certain number of failed log-in attempts.

CHAPTER 6

Personal data breaches

Prevention is better than cure, according to the old proverb. In other words, it is much easier to stop something from happening in the first place than having to repair the damage afterwards.

In the case of personal data breaches it is a question of:

1 the steps you can and should take in order to minimise the risks of a data breach occurring (see Chapter 5)
2 using data protection impact assessments (see Chapter 10) before the introduction of a new library service or the modification of an existing one where it is likely to result in a high risk to the rights and freedoms of individuals. The purpose of the DPIA is to evaluate the origin, nature, particularity and severity of the risk and to identify the measures that will need to be taken to mitigate that risk before any processing is undertaken.
3 If any data breaches do occur, however big or small, it is important to learn any lessons from those breaches by modifying the library's processes and procedures to address any weaknesses or vulnerabilities uncovered by your investigations.

This chapter looks at how to respond when a breach has been identified, or is suspected to have taken place. It looks at the need for a data breach response plan, deciding whether the breach is serious enough to trigger the legal requirement to notify the Information Commissioner's Office, and the affected individuals. It also considers the need for a communications strategy.

The chapter sets out a number of library-related examples of personal data breaches and their causes.

A personal data breach is defined in the GDPR as 'a breach of security leading to the accidental or unlawful destruction, loss, alteration, unauthorised disclosure of, or access to, personal data transmitted, stored or otherwise processed' (Article 4(12)).

The definition encompasses breaches that are the result of both accidental and deliberate causes and it also encompasses more breaches than just those that are about losing personal data.

The CIA triad of **c**onfidentiality, **i**ntegrity and **a**vailability is at the heart of information security:

- **Confidentiality** is a set of rules that limits access to information.
- **Integrity** is the assurance that the information is trustworthy and accurate.
- **Availability** is a guarantee of reliable access to the information by authorised people.

A personal data breach seen through the CIA triad is a security incident that affects the confidentiality, integrity or availability of personal data. Examples of what the CIA triad covers are shown in Table 6.1.

Table 6.1 *The CIA information security triad – what it covers and examples*

CIA triad	What it covers	Example
Confidentiality breach	Where there is an authorised or accidental disclosure of, or access to, personal data	Allowing the same information to appear in far too many places (thereby increasing the risk of disclosure)
Integrity breach	Where there is an unauthorised or accidental alteration of personal data	Where the personal data has been corrupted
Availability breach	Where there is an accidental or unauthorised loss of access to, or destruction of, personal data	Where the personal data has been encrypted by ransomware, or accidentally lost or destroyed

6.1   Personal data breach response plan

It is important to have a data breach response plan in place which sets out the procedures to follow and the clear lines of authority for library staff in the event that the library experiences a personal data breach, or suspects that a personal data breach has taken place.

Data breaches can be caused or exacerbated by a range of factors; they can affect different types of personally identifiable information; they can affect different categories of individuals; and they can give rise to a range of potential or actual harms to individuals.

Having a data breach response plan in place will help the library to quickly contain, assess and respond to a data breach if one has been detected. It will help mitigate any potential harms to the affected individuals; and it will also help the library to ensure compliance with the GDPR's notification requirements.

You should ensure you have robust breach detection, investigation and reporting procedures (both internally and externally) in place. This will facilitate decision making about whether or not you need to notify the relevant supervisory authority and the affected individuals.

The five key steps to consider when dealing with a breach or suspected breach are shown in Figure 6.1.

Step 1	Identify
Step 2	Contain
Step 3	Investigate
Step 4	Notify
Step 5	Review

Figure 6.1 *Five-step data breach response plan*

6.1.1   Implementing the five-step plan
Step 1: *Identify* the breach

Consider how you will detect or be alerted to a personal data breach:

1 internally notified:
   - monitoring tools
   - library staff reporting
2 externally notified:
   - library users
   - the supervisory authority (the ICO)
   - partners and vendors
3 contacted by the perpetrator:
   - extortion attempts by the hacker
   - ransom demands by the hacker.

Step 2: *Contain* the breach

- Notify the data controller and the data protection officer, who may convene the data breach response team.
- Immediately contain the data breach (i.e. turn off any system that is causing a breach, attempt to retract e-mails that shouldn't have been sent, etc.).
- Secure and isolate affected systems to limit further data loss.
- If possible the library should prevent the likely risk of serious harm through remedial action.
- Preserve evidence. This may prove invaluable in establishing the cause of the breach and/or allow the organisation to take appropriate corrective action.
- Convene the data breach response team in accordance with this plan.

Step 3: *Investigate* the breach and the associated risks to the rights and freedoms of individuals

- Conduct initial investigation, and gather information about the breach promptly, including:

- the date, time, duration and location of the breach
- the type of personal information involved in the breach
- how the breach was identified and by whom
- a list of the affected individuals, or possibly affected individuals
- the risk of harms (and their seriousness) to the affected individuals.
- Analyse and establish the cause and extent of the breach; and systems affected.
- Assess priorities and risks based on what is known.
- Keep appropriate records:
  - description of the breach
  - the actions and decisions of the data breach response team
  - the steps taken to rectify the situation
  - all your findings
  - if the data controller decides no further action is required, the reasons for that view.

Step 4: _Notify_ (fulfil breach notification requirements)

- Determine whether there are any legal requirements to notify the breach:
  - to the ICO within 72 hours (where there is a risk to the rights and freedoms of individuals)
  - to the affected individuals (where there is a high risk to their rights and freedoms).
- Inform the ICO as soon as possible. Provide ongoing updates on key developments if required.
- Even if the legal threshold for notification has not been met, consider whether you ought to notify anyone (including stakeholders, partners, vendors).
- Consider your approach to informing people about the breach, in accordance with your communications strategy.

Step 5: _Review_ the incident and take remedial action to prevent future breaches

- Remove known vulnerabilities.
- Repair systems, having fully investigated the cause of the breach.
- Identify and address any weaknesses in data handling that contributed to the breach.
- Conduct a post-breach review and report your recommendations to library trustees.
- Make appropriate changes to policies and procedures if necessary.
- Does the breach point to a systemic problem in the library's processes or procedures?
- Revise staff training practices if required.

- Update the data breach response plan if required.
- Consider the option of an audit to ensure necessary outcomes are effected.

6.1.2 Testing the personal data breach response plan

Members of the data breach response team should test the data breach response plan using an imaginary data breach. This should happen on an annual basis in order to ensure that the plan is effective. The outcome of the test should be made available to the library trustees, along with any recommendations for improving the plan.

6.2 Communications strategy

It is important to have a communications strategy in place, and to establish consistent methods for communication. The legislation requires that personal data breaches are reported **without undue delay** and, where feasible, **not later than 72 hours after becoming aware of the breach.**

Processor organisations in practice need to have protocols between the parties for public announcements about a security break. The parties will in many cases want to agree those protocols in a written agreement.

Where you outsource the processing of personal data to other companies, you will be considered to be aware of any data breaches as soon as the processor themselves recognises that a breach has taken place.

6.2.1 Documenting personal data breaches

Data controllers are required to document *any* personal data breaches, regardless of whether there is a requirement to report them or not. The documentary record of the data breach should comprise the facts relating to the personal data breach, its effects and the remedial action taken. That documentation will enable the supervisory authority to verify compliance with Article 33 of the GDPR.

The DPO should have an incident register with all breaches or incidents recorded, even if they are 'low-risk'. This will enable them to identify patterns such as a particular department regularly reporting incidents, which may require more training, or repeated breaches of the same nature, for example auto-fill of e-mail address, meaning e-mails containing personal data are sent to the wrong person – this may require the auto-fill function to be switched off, perhaps for certain teams who handle sensitive information, in order to reduce the risk of data breaches occurring.

6.2.2 Notification of a personal data breach to the supervisory authority (GDPR Article 33)

The GDPR introduces a duty on all organisations to report certain types of personal data breach to the relevant supervisory authority (in the UK that is the Information Commissioner's Office (ICO)).

Article 33 of the GDPR outlines the requirements for notifying the supervisory authority of personal data breaches, while Article 34 covers communication of a personal data breach to the data subject.

Where a personal data breach occurs the controller shall **without undue delay** and, where feasible, **not later than 72 hours after becoming aware of the breach** notify the Information Commissioner's Office. The requirement to notify the ICO applies unless the personal data breach is unlikely to result in a risk to the rights and freedoms of natural persons.

Where you don't have full and comprehensive details of the incident it is possible to provide the information to the ICO in phases. In those circumstances, the data controller should notify the ICO of the personal data breach as soon as they possibly can, even if they only have a limited amount of information about the breach at that stage, and then provide additional information as it becomes available.

If the notification to the supervisory authority is not made within 72 hours, it should be accompanied by reasons for the delay.

Data controllers have ultimate responsibility for the processing of personal data. They may undertake the processing of that data either alone or jointly with others. Where a data processor processes personal data on behalf of the controller, the data processor has a direct responsibility to notify any personal data breaches to the data controller. They should do so without undue delay after becoming aware of a personal data breach. But legal responsibility to report the data breach to the ICO (and, where appropriate the affected individuals) remains with the data controller.

GDPR Article 33 sets out the information that should be provided in the notification to the supervisory authority (in the UK that is the ICO). The notification should at least:

(a) describe the nature of the personal data breach including, where possible, the categories and approximate number of data subjects concerned and the categories and approximate number of personal data records concerned
(b) communicate the name and contact details of the data protection officer or other contact point where more information can be obtained
(c) describe the likely consequences of the personal data breach
(d) describe the measures taken or proposed to be taken by the controller to address the personal data breach, including, where appropriate, measures to mitigate its possible adverse effects.

6.2.3   Communication of a personal data breach to the data subject (GDPR Article 34)

The controller should, without undue delay, communicate to the individuals whose data has been the subject of a personal data breach where that personal data breach is likely to result in a **high** risk to the rights and freedoms of the natural person, in order to allow him or her to take the necessary precautions.

The communication should describe the nature of the personal data breach as well as recommendations for what the individual concerned can do to mitigate potential adverse effects. Such communications to data subjects should be made as soon as reasonably feasible and in close co-operation with the supervisory authority, respecting guidance provided by it or by other relevant authorities such as law enforcement authorities.

The communication to the data subject shall describe in clear and plain language the nature of the personal data breach and contain at least the information and measures referred to in points (b), (c) and (d) above.

It is not necessary to send a communication to the data subject about a personal data breach if any of the following conditions are met:

(a) the controller has implemented appropriate technical and organisational protection measures, and those measures were applied to the personal data affected by the personal data breach, in particular those that render the personal data unintelligible to any person who is not authorised to access it, such as encryption

(b) the controller has taken subsequent measures which ensure that the high risk to the rights and freedoms of data subjects is no longer likely to materialise

(c) it would involve disproportionate effort. In such a case, there shall instead be a public communication or similar measure whereby the data subjects are informed in an equally effective manner.

Figure 6.2 on the next page gives an example of what a personal data breach notification policy should look like.

6.3   Payment card data

If you process payment card data and suffer a personal data breach, the ICO will consider the extent to which you have put in place measures that the Payment Card Industry Data Security Standard requires, particularly if the breach related to a lack of a particular control or process mandated by the standard. The GDPR specifically requires you to have a process for regularly testing, assessing and evaluating the effectiveness of any measures you put in place.

Whatever form of testing you undertake, you should document the results

Nowheresville Public Library Personal Data Breach Notification Policy

This policy defines the circumstances under which the Nowheresville Public Library shall provide notice regarding a breach in security leading to the accidental or unlawful destruction, loss, alteration, unauthorised disclosure of, or access to, personal data transmitted, stored or otherwise processed.

This policy applies to information stored by the Nowheresville Public Library. Suspected or confirmed personal data breaches must be reported immediately to the Library Director.

The library will investigate all reports of breaches of security related to personal data maintained by the library. Based on the results of the investigation, internal and/or external parties may be notified, as necessary.

Upon notification of a suspected information security breach, the library will:

- Report the breach to the appropriate people (to the ICO where there is a risk to the rights and freedoms of individuals; and to the affected individuals where there is a high risk to the rights and freedoms of those individuals)
- Block, mitigate, or de-escalate the breach, if possible
- Repair systems and remove known vulnerabilities
- Implement processes and procedures to prevent similar breaches from occurring in future.

If a breach is suspected to have taken place the following information will be required in order to assess the seriousness of the breach:

- The type of data involved
- Whether the breach involves sensitive personal data
- If the data has been lost or stolen, whether there are any protections in place such as encryption
- What has happened to the data
- What the data could tell a third party about an individual
- The volume of data (how many individuals' personal data is affected by the breach)
- Who are the individuals whose data has been breached
- What harm can come to those individuals.

Internal Notification

The person discovering the breach will report it to the Library Director, who will establish an appropriate response strategy. The Library Director will inform the Library's Board of Trustees and, where appropriate, the organisation's in-house lawyer.

External Notification

The Library Director will determine whether the conditions laid out in the GDPR requiring external notification have been triggered:

- Notifying the Information Commissioner's Office within 72 hours where the personal data breach is likely to result in a risk to the rights and freedoms of individuals
- Where the notification to the ICO is not made within 72 hours, it shall be accompanied by reasons for the delay.

The individuals affected will be notified without undue delay where there is a high risk to their rights and freedoms. The notification will describe in clear and plain language the nature of the breach, in order to allow them to take the necessary precautions.

Adopted 15 January 2020.

Figure 6.2 *Example of a personal data breach notification policy*

and make sure that you act upon any recommendations, or have a valid reason for not doing so, and implement appropriate safeguards. This is particularly important if your testing reveals potential critical flaws that could result in a personal data breach.

6.4 Library examples of personal data breaches

6.4.1 Leaked e-mails reveal what a politician borrowed from the library

Hillary Clinton's e-mails from her term as US Secretary of State were leaked. The e-mails show a list of books that she requested her staff borrow from the library for her to browse. They include a book of poetry and a memoir, as well as books on the CIA, climate change and US history (Ha, 2016).

6.4.2 Newspaper publishes details of books borrowed by famous writer

Japanese librarians accused a newspaper of violating the privacy of Haruki Murakami, Japan's best-known contemporary writer, when it revealed his teenage reading habits (McCurry, 2015).

6.4.3 Inadvertent data breach relating to a library user

A library staff member inadvertently mentioned the name of another library user to a library user she was serving (they knew each other). No disciplinary action was taken (BigBrotherWatch, 2015).

6.4.4 Data breach at university library

Students at Trinity College Dublin were warned that some of their data may have been compromised after a breach at the college's library. A file containing student and staff names, addresses, ID numbers and e-mail addresses was inadvertently made accessible on the college network. Students were warned to look out for phishing or spam e-mails as a result of the breach (McLysaght, 2011).

6.4.5 Failed attempt to obtain library customer data

During 2015/16 the British Library withstood a 'brute force' attack on its systems over a four-day period, in which the attacker attempted to obtain access to customer data. The attack was unsuccessful and no data was lost (British Library, 2016).

6.4.6   Social security numbers in library books

Years ago students and faculty at some American libraries would put their names and sometimes their social security numbers on the cards in books.

> The university (of Toledo) recently discovered books in circulation with borrowers' personal information. . . . It only took a couple of minutes to locate a book with a social security number in the sciences section of the Carlson Library. Social security numbers were listed right next to the borrowers' names.
>
> (Miller, 2009)

6.4.7   Lost USB stick containing sensitive data accessed in a library

An employee at Heathrow Airport lost a memory stick containing over 1,000 files which were neither encrypted nor password protected. The files included a training video that revealed ten individuals' personal details, including names, dates of birth, passport numbers, along with the details of up to 50 Heathrow Airport aviation security staff. The contents of the memory stick were viewed by a member of the public at a library (Archer, 2018). The information on the USB stick included the locations of every CCTV camera at the airport, routes and security protection measures for VIPs, and maps of the airport's tunnels and escape shafts (Gallagher, 2017). The Information Commissioner's Office fined Heathrow Airport £120,000 for failing to secure sensitive personal data (Archer, 2018).

6.4.8   Reviews and ratings on library website

> The new Multnomah County Library website is designed to let you post reviews and ratings of items in the library collection, similar to Amazon.com. Unfortunately, it does so at the cost of your privacy. To use the new website, you will have to surrender confidential information, including your name, date of birth, e-mail address, and a list of all the items you have checked out, to a Canadian company, BiblioCommons. By contracting with a foreign company, the library has avoided Oregon privacy laws and given this information to a company that is out of the reach of most Oregonians. In effect, you are required to surrender private data to a foreign company in order to use a government service.
>
> (Greiner, 2013)

6.4.9   Librarian sues Equifax over data breach

Vermont librarian Jessamyn West sued Equifax over its 2017 data breach and won $600 in the small claims court. Just days after Equifax disclosed the breach, West filed a claim with the local Orange County, VT, courthouse asking a judge to award her almost $5,000. She told the court that her mother had just died in July, and that it added to the work of sorting out her mom's finances while trying to respond to having the entire family's credit files potentially exposed to hackers and identity thieves. The judge ultimately agreed, but awarded West just $690 ($90 to cover court fees and the rest intended to cover the cost of up to two years of payments to online identity theft protection services).

6.5 Causes of data breaches

Personal data breaches can be caused either by inadequate security technology and/or by organisational, process and people failures, for example:

- negligent insiders
- malicious insiders
- external attackers
- physical loss:
  - lost or stolen data/hardware
  - lost in transit
- social engineering/'phishing'
- failure to fully implement purchased security products
- IT configuration errors
- disclosed in error
- non-secure disposal.

There are a wide range of potential risks that can arise through a data breach, including financial loss, fines from the regulator, reputational loss, loss of business systems, lost productivity, loss of intellectual property and legal costs.

Table 6.2 lists some common causes of data breaches with examples of how these have occurred in libraries.

Table 6.2 *Examples of library-related personal data breaches*

Causes of data breaches	Library-related example
Software upgrade glitch	Confidential information for around 126,000 students and employees at six community colleges in Florida was publicly available on the internet, according to the College Center for Library Automation. Students reported finding personal information through a Google search. The breach happened as a result of a software upgrade (Travis, 2010).

Continued

Table 6.2 *Continued*

Causes of data breaches	Library-related example
Misconfigured database	San Diego State University discovered that a database which had been set up and managed by the Pre-College Institute, containing names, social security numbers, dates of birth, addresses and other personal information, had been misconfigured, thereby enabling any computer connected to the SDSU-wired network with the program 'File Maker' to access the information (Gough, 2014).
Insider threat • negligent insiders (see British Information Industry Association (BIIA), 2016) • dishonest/malicious insiders	A man who worked in the human resources department of the Library of Congress used a government database to obtain the names, birthdates and social security numbers of at least ten library employees. He passed the information on to a relative who used the stolen identities of the federal workers to open credit accounts at major retailers, buying thousands of dollars' worth of goods (Wilber, 2008).
Hacking attack • SQL injection • session hijacking • packet sniffing	On 7 October 2014 the server running Wyoming's statewide online library catalogue WYLDCat was breached by unknown intruders based outside the USA. Borrower records containing personally identifying information may have been accessed (Price, 2014).
DDOS attack	In July 2016 there was a denial of service attack on the Library of Congress which caused a three-day service outage. According to Bernbach (2016) it 'validated decades of complaints about the Library of Congress's failure to join the digital age'. The attack affected library operations including internal websites and employee e-mail. DDOS attacks are becoming a routine strategy used by cybercriminals intent on committing fraud or extortion.

Continued

Table 6.2 *Continued*

Causes of data breaches	Library-related example
Computing devices containing personal data being lost or stolen	Library Systems & Services LLC discovered that a laptop had been lost or stolen on 5 November 2012. The laptop may have contained employee names, social security numbers, addresses, and dates of birth (Privacy Rights Clearinghouse, 2012).
Keystroke logging software	Keyloggers which record keyboard activity were found by staff on the back of two PCs at Wilmslow Library and one at Handforth Library. Two of the devices were confiscated by staff, but the third had been removed before a supervisor got to it (BBC News Online, 2011).
Alteration of personal data without permission	A library staff member inadvertently came across the borrower record of a library user which contained data entries of a highly inappropriate, sexually explicit nature. It was not possible to determine who had edited the record in this manner because library staff regularly used generic library staff log-ins (see case study of Ireland Sierra LMS in Chapter 4, p. 76).
Sending personal data to an incorrect recipient	A member of the committee of a library-related special interest group sent an e-mail out to group members without using the blind copy (BCC) facility. In doing so they unintentionally allowed everyone to see each others' e-mail addresses.
Loss of availability of personal data	On 26 January 2016 Lincolnshire County Council was subject to a malware attack on its IT system (Lincolnshire County Council, 2016). One consequence of this was that computers could not be used in libraries. Data was unavailable as a result of being encrypted by ransomware.

Continued

Table 6.2 *Continued*

Causes of data breaches	Library-related example
Access by an unauthorised third party	For almost 31 hours over Labor Day weekend in 2015, the American Library Association's Facebook page was controlled by a hacker who posted decidedly un-library-like content and removed all ALA admins. While ALA's Social Media Team scrambled to find a way to regain access to the page, new spam posts were going up every 20 minutes like clockwork (Coleman and Levine, 2015).
Security breaches due to human error	A library-related entity published the results of a survey. They 'anonymised' the data whilst forgetting to remove the field for IP address. Anyone who wanted to could use a reverse search tool to find the organisation to which the IP addresses belong.

Bert-Jaap Koops from the Tilburg Law School wrote (Koops, 2011) of the internet having an 'iron memory', with access to mountains of data on any given topic, and how pieces of data could be categorised as either digital footprints (data created by the individual), or data shadows (data generated about individuals by others).

Wharton (2018, 42) makes the point that when discussing privacy and ethics, the concern for information professionals resides in the risk of *future* harm to users. This is an interesting point, because we are all building up a 'digital footprint' or trail as we go about our daily lives. A digital footprint is the data you leave behind when you go online. It's what you've said, what others have said about you, where you've been, images you're tagged in, personal information, social media profiles and much more. Wharton's point about future harms is important because it is impossible to fully understand the potential future harms that can be caused by breaches of personal data. A few pieces of personally identifiable information taken one by one might not seem to be too problematic. But what if they are taken together; what if they are later combined with yet more of your personal data as the trail consisting of both your digital footprint and your data shadows grows? And what about the increasing capabilities of the technology and its capacity to analyse and process that data in ways you had never anticipated?

When one tries to assess the potential effects of a data breach, one should take into account what is known as the mosaic effect - the features within a dataset that, in combination with other data, identify individuals.

Innocuous traces of everyday life submitted to sophisticated analytics tools developed for commerce and governance can become the keys for stitching disparate databases together into unprecedented new wholes.

(Brunton and Nissenbaum, 2013)

One way of limiting the potential risks for a library as the data controller is to limit the amount of personal data that you collect, known as 'data minimisation'. Another is to keep the personal data only for as long as you need it.

In Germany *Datensparsamkeit* (which translates as 'data economy' or 'data thrift', and is another way of expressing the concept of data minimisation) is enshrined in section 71 of the Federal Data Protection Act (*Bundesdatenschutzgesetz* or BDSG), which came into force on 25 May 2018. This sets a requirement in particular to align the processing of personal data and the selection and design of data processing systems with the goal of processing as little personal data as possible. In addition, personal data must be anonymised or pseudonymised at the earliest possible date, as far as this is possible according to the purpose of the processing (Bundesministerium der Justiz und für Verbraucherschutz, 2017).

➜ Personal data breach checklist

- Do we have a response plan for addressing any personal data breaches that occur?
- Have we allocated responsibility for managing breaches to a dedicated person or team (a data breach incident response team)?
- Do library staff know how to escalate a security incident to the appropriate person or team within the library service (or parent organisation) to determine whether a breach has occurred?

CHAPTER 7

Access to and sharing of user data

7.1 Responding to requests for patron records

Attempts to gain access to patron records may come from many different sources. For example, they could come from a parent wanting to know what his/her child is reading, or from a member of a university department trying to find out whether a student has checked out a book she or he is suspected of plagiarising. Indeed, requests could come from a wide range of sources such as the police, from journalists, from students, from teachers, or from other family members.

This is where it is important to have a privacy policy statement which covers the sharing of library user records. Faced with a request from a husband asking about the borrowing record of his wife the librarian will have a clear set of guidelines that they are working to, and can point the requester to the library's privacy policy.

More problematic are requests for access to library user records from the police. In the USA the American Library Association has produced guidance on how to respond to such requests (American Library Association, 2017). US librarians normally won't give out information about library users under any circumstances, except where a proper court order has been presented.

The police can request patron data from UK public libraries. The problem is that in the UK there are a number of different ways in which the police have the powers to obtain library user records, and not all of them require a court order. One route would be to make a request to the data protection officer under Schedule 2 Part 1 Paragraph 2 of DPA 2018, which gives them an exemption from GDPR for requesting personal information for the purpose of detecting crime. It would then be up to the DPO to determine if the justification the police gave was sufficient to justify releasing personal information, i.e. whether it was clear that the police could not access this information by any other means and that the information requested would directly assist the detection or prevention of crime.

In the case of RIPA requests for covert human intelligence sources (CHIS), the authorisation can be from a senior member of the authority. In the case of the police 'a superintendent or an assistant chief constable (for relevant sources) can authorise the conduct of a CHIS, but an authorisation for *intrusive* surveillance by the police needs the separate authorisation of a chief constable (and the prior approval of a Judicial Commissioner, except in cases of urgency)' (Home Office, 2018, 18). According to Nelson (2014), anti-terror laws are being used to suck in sensitive data without the traditional protections. RIPA was passed in the name of fighting terrorism, but as Nelson suggests, it has been used more broadly by the police in order to gather information. Nelson points out that the only check for police using snooping powers is the Investigatory Powers Tribunal, which does not allow complainants to know why they were targeted in the first place. In 14 years it upheld just 14 complaints.

Does your library have a clear policy in place setting out how to respond to requests for patron records? Figure 7.1 illustrates the kind of data-sharing policy a library may have in place.

Who will have access to your information?
The Data Controller for your information is Nowheresville Council.
E-mail: dataprotection@nowheresville.gov.uk

SirsiDynix (Symphony) are our data processors – we use their software systems to manage Nowheresville Public Library (NPL) information. The data is kept in secure environments on servers outside NPL. The data processors hold contracts with Nowheresville Council and are bound by data protection legislation and by the contract to protect your personal information.

SirsiDynix for the Symphony Library Management System, has a privacy statement at www.sirsidynix.com/privacy.

Once your information has been collected by Nowheresville Council, it may be used by other local authority members of the London Libraries Consortium, where necessary, to provide a complete service to you across London. This will save you providing the information multiple times if you live, study or work across London.

These are the organisations we share your data with:

Library Management System (SirsiDynix Symphony)	Personal information to provide access to library resources
Debt collection	Contact and finance information will be shared for debt collection
Online resource providers: Bolinda (Borrow Box) RB Digital (E-Zines, Comics Plus, E-Audio, E-books) ABC self-service machines	Name and library card number to provide authorised access to Nowheresville Public Library's purchased licences
Other local authority members of the London Libraries Consortium	All data as part of the London-wide library provision, allowing access to libraries where you live, study and work without the need to duplicate input
Other Nowheresville Council departments	Contact and personal information in relation to safeguarding issues
Police	Contact and personal information, on request

We would only share your personally identifiable information in any other way if required by law to do so, or if additional consent from you had been obtained.

Figure 7.1 *Example of a library data-sharing policy*

Thinking about the sort of policy a library service that participates in a consortium might have, this could make clear that:

- Each authority is required on joining the consortium to complete a Data Protection Impact Assessment and notify customers (through website, posters, leaflets etc.) that their details may be shared amongst the participating authorities.
- Library users may choose to opt out of this, but they would then be unable to take full advantage of the shared services, such as cross-authority item requests.

All staff should be trained on the library's policy for responding to requests for patron records. Before any personally identifiable information is shared in response to a court order or search warrant, the chief librarian/library director should be informed. Library staff should take formal legal advice on what they may be legally obliged to share.

7.1.1   What records are you being asked to share?

Requests may come:

- from library users:
  - the data subject
  - other library users
- from law enforcement agencies:
  - with a court order (ask for a copy of the court order; closely examine scope - exact premises to be searched, exactly what is to be seized; be careful not to consent to a broader search)
  - without a court order (verbal requests, written requests).

You may be asked for: library user records (circulation history, library registration record, browser history, etc.); or other information about the user (what you saw them accessing on screen, description of their behaviour or other information obtained through observation by library staff or volunteers). As a precaution, consider taking pictures to record the event taking place, keep copies of items seized and write your own inventory of items seized.

Is the request for patron data subject to any form of gagging order, where no one is permitted to disclose that law enforcement authorities have sought or obtained library user data?

7.2   Examples of where library user data was accessed by third parties

7.2.1   London Bridge terrorist

A number of library cards taken out at Dublin libraries by the London Bridge terrorist Rachid Redouane were reviewed in a bid to uncover information about his life in Ireland (Lally, 2017). These library cards included several temporary visitor cards as well as one for permanent membership of a library in Dublin's inner city. 'Internet searches at the libraries on the dates he registered for the cards could now be checked in a bid to determine whether, for example, any extremist material was being viewed on those dates and perhaps who he was in touch with' (Lally, 2017).

7.2.2   Murder of Jo Cox MP

Jo Cox was murdered on 16 June 2016 as she was on her way to a library where she was about to hold a surgery in her Yorkshire constituency. Police seized computers at Birstall Library. In the trial of Thomas Mair – the man who was found guilty of the MP's murder – the jury were told that the previous evening Mair had been to the library and had looked up the Wikipedia page for the 'Occidental Observer'. 'The page states that it is a far-right publication with a white nationalist and anti-semitic perspective, and which is concerned with matters such as white identity and western culture' (Cobain, 2016). Two days earlier, at the same library, Mair had viewed Cox's Twitter feed, the court heard. According to Kirk (2016) he had also used his local library to research Ms Cox, fellow Yorkshire MP William Hague, and Ian Gow, an MP murdered by the Provisional IRA.

7.3   Potential risks in releasing datasets for open data initiatives

Librarians naturally want to provide access to information. They see that as being central to their role as information professionals. In light of this, they see the sharing of information through open data initiatives as being a good thing. Their rationale for doing so is premised on the data that is released either not containing any personally identifiable information, or where it does, ensuring that this is fully anonymised. Library and information professionals take that stance because of the way in which they enable access to information whilst simultaneously recognising the need to protect the personal data, and particularly the sensitive personal data, of their library users.

The problem, as noted by Rubinstein (2013), is that big data calls into question the distinction between personal and non-personal data. Big data can include data from both and through sophisticated data mining techniques combine them to form new data that may not be labelled as personal data, and thus avoid regulation. Yet this data can still be applied to and affect individuals.

Green et al. (2017) provide a very good example of how the release of seemingly innocuous data can have serious implications. Their example covers open city data, and illustrates very well the reasons why the potential dangers arising from *future* harms need to be taken fully into account whenever new datasets are released.

In response to a freedom of information (FOI) request, New York City's Taxi and Limousine Commission released data detailing every taxi ride recorded in registered NYC taxis in 2013. The data contained information about: pick-up time and location; drop-off time and location; fare and tip amount; and anonymised (hashed) versions of the taxi's licence and medallion number. Green et al. note that one data scientist was able to use this information to re-identify the drivers involved in every trip.

Meanwhile, another data scientist, Anthony Tockar, took the taxi data and analysed the patterns of trips. He was able to demonstrate how the dataset could be used to reveal not just the identities of the taxi drivers, but that it could also go well beyond this to reveal sensitive personal data about the passengers. Tockar (2014) focused on studying the behavioural trends of visitors to a strip club in New York City. He mapped out the drop-off location of every taxi trip that began outside one specific strip club. By looking for the locations at which many taxi trips ended, he was able to identify where frequent visitors lived. Because the geographic co-ordinates were given with such precision, Tockar was able to pinpoint certain individuals with a high degree of probability. This information was then combined with auxiliary information available online to make re-identification possible.

Before data is released as part of an open data initiative, one consideration that should be taken into account is the possibility of re-identification through shared fields in multiple datasets. In order to assess the potential risks involved, it is essential to factor in not only the datasets that are already in the public domain, but also any that are likely to become publicly available in the foreseeable future; and also to consider the likelihood of the re-identification risks becoming significantly greater as a result of the ever-increasing analytical capabilities of the technology. Anytime a dataset shares certain data fields with another dataset, there is the chance that one could use those fields to crosswalk between datasets.

Sometimes libraries share information quite innocently, but realise later that there might be privacy concerns:

• Parry (2012) tells of how Harvard librarians set up Twitter feeds broadcasting titles of books being checked out from campus libraries. Even though the Twitter stream randomised checkout times and did not disclose patrons' identities, nevertheless privacy concerns were raised because the worry was that someone might somehow use other details to identify the borrowers.

- Warren (2016) tells of how Toronto Public Library was revealing its website searches in real time. The library had developed a tool using Google Analytics to pull search topics into one place. This provided a window into the range of interests and needs people bring to the library, or as Warren puts it 'offering a fascinating glimpse into the city's psyche'.

Figure 7.2 lists some considerations on the risk of releasing open data.

• What datasets are already in the public domain?
• What datasets are likely to be released into the public domain in the foreseeable future?
• Are there any fields in the dataset to be released that are shared with other publicly available datasets?
• What are the risks of a combination of data being used to re-identify library users?
• Is the distinction between personal and non-personal data clear-cut, bearing in mind the availability of sophisticated data mining techniques?

Figure 7.2 *What to consider before releasing datasets as open data*

CHAPTER 8

Privacy policy statements

A privacy policy statement, or privacy notice, is a document that is used to set out the data controllers' policies on how they process the data that is within their control. Providing accessible information to individuals about the use of their personal information is a key element of the General Data Protection Regulation and sets a legal framework with which libraries must comply. Thinking about your library's privacy policy, ask yourself:

• How easy is the policy to read?
• How long does it take to read?
• How clearly does it explain how personal information is handled?
• Does it cover everything the GDPR requires?

A good privacy notice will:

• be written in clear language the data subject will understand
• be truthful and unambiguous
• highlight any changes made to the way the personal data is processed
• be easily accessible to library users.

The main purpose of a privacy policy should be to inform the public, rather than being primarily a means for organisations to protect themselves. In reality privacy policy statements often simply disclose some or all of the ways in which the website collects, retains and shares personal data with third parties. Privacy policy statements are therefore something of a misnomer, because what they actually do is to set out the ways in which users' personal data is neither private nor under their control.

If a library user wants to make an informed choice about whether they can trust the library to protect their privacy, they need to read more than just the library's own privacy policy. Libraries rely on technology and content providers in order to be able to deliver their services. To be fully informed, library users would also need to read the privacy policies of each of the library's vendors.

According to TOSDR (Terms Of Service Didn't Read, https://tosdr.org), 'I have read and agree to the Terms' is the biggest lie on the web. The TOSDR service picks out the key points from sets of terms and conditions for sites such as Google, YouTube, Trello, eBay, Amazon, Twitch, Twitter, Instagram, Bing and Microsoft Store. TOSDR summarises the terms and conditions of websites in plain English. When people click 'I agree to these terms and conditions', they rarely read through them. According to Obar and Oeldorf-Hirsch (2016) who, upon discussing terms of service with their colleagues, found that most agreed that ignoring terms of service policies are both a reality and a problem, 'I never read those things' and 'nobody reads them' are common responses. TOSDR aim to fix that. The site rates and labels website terms and privacy policies from very good (categorised as Class A) to very bad (categorised as Class E). They use symbols to indicate which points in the terms and conditions are positive and which are negative, as well as highlighting key points to note. TOSDR has a web browser add-on which makes it possible to get the ratings directly into your browser.

It is useful to look at some of the T&C summaries because they flag up many of the sorts of issues that should be covered in a library privacy policy, for example:

- if the service uses tracking pixels, web beacons, browser fingerprinting and/or device fingerprinting
- the involvement of third parties in operating the service
- that personal data is used for limited purposes
- only necessary user logs are kept by the service to ensure quality
- the service shows the date of the last time the T&Cs were updated.

The TOSDR project was started in June 2012. TOSDR believe that almost no one really reads the terms of service that they agree to all the time. This is hardly surprising, given the length of some of them; given the use of legal jargon rather than plain English; and given the number of sites that the average user is likely to encounter on a daily basis. Nevertheless, the terms and privacy policies are important to understand. The rights of you and your users depend on precisely what is in those sets of T&Cs.

8.1   What the privacy policy notice should cover

Under the transparency provisions of the GDPR, the information you need to give people includes:

- the purposes of your processing
- the categories of personal data concerned
- the lawful basis for processing the data
- the recipients or categories of recipient you disclose the personal data to and why
- what those recipients will do with the data

- your retention period for storing the personal data or, where this is not possible, your criteria for determining how long you will store it
- the existence of their right to request access to, rectification, erasure or restriction, or to object to such processing, as well as the right to data portability
- the right to lodge a complaint with the ICO
- information about the source of the data, where it was not obtained directly from the individual
- the existence of automated decision making (including profiling):
  - in those cases, meaningful information about the logic involved, as well as the significance and the envisaged consequences of such processing for the data subject
- the safeguards you provide if you transfer personal data to a third country or international organisation
- the identity and the contact details of the controller
- the contact details of the data protection officer
- where controllers say the processing is necessary for the purposes of their legitimate interests, the detail of this
- where the processing is based on data subjects having given consent to that processing, the existence of their right to withdraw consent at any time
- where the controller intends to further process the personal data for a purpose other than that for which the personal data were collected, the controller shall provide the data subject prior to that further processing with information on that other purpose.

8.2   Children and the age of consent

Persons giving consent need to have a certain level of understanding of what they are being asked, which is why the GDPR specifies that parents or guardians must give consent to personal data processing on behalf of young children using information society services. 'Information society services' generally include commercial websites. The term is defined as any service normally provided for remuneration, at a distance, by electronic means and at the individual request of a recipient of services (see Article 1(1)(b) of EU Directive 2015/1535).

The default age of consent in the GDPR is 16. However, the GDPR allows the UK to set the threshold for the minimum age at which a child can consent to such data processing to any age between 13 years and 16 years, and the UK has chosen 13 as the age of consent, although the situation in Scotland is slightly different. Section 208 of the DPA 2018 provides that in Scotland a child under 16 can exercise their rights or give consent under the data protection legislation if the child understands what it means to exercise that right or give such consent. A person aged 12 or over is to be presumed to be of sufficient age and maturity to have such understanding unless it is proved otherwise.

A library privacy policy may include a statement along the lines:

> We require signed parental consent for children under 13 to enable the library to hold and share their data on the library management system and to share with partners. If you are accessing online services and are under the age of 13, please get your parent/guardian's permission beforehand whenever you provide us with personal information.

8.3   Cookie policy

Library web pages use internet cookies. Cookies are small files that function in the background of a website. They often include unique identifiers sent by web servers to web browsers, and which may then be sent back to the server each time the browser requests a page from the server. Cookies can be used by web servers to identify and track users as they navigate different pages on a website, and to identify users returning to a website.

Cookies can allow recent search history and preferences to be retrieved for quicker and easier web browsing, and websites are customised based on past preferences.

A library privacy policy statement should make clear if cookies are used on the library's website. For example, it might say:

> We use cookies for the following functions:
>
> - to remember that the user has closed the 'This site uses cookies...' message
> - to track page usage and visitor profiles, the results of which are used to inform future development of the website.
>
> None of these cookies tracks your browsing behaviour beyond this website and they do not gather personal information.

8.3.1   Types of cookie

There are a number of different types of cookie (see Table 8.1). A key distinction is that between first-party cookies and third-party cookies. If a library website allows 'third-party cookies', this can have a significant impact on privacy. Third-party cookies enable commercial entities to 'scoop up' our preferences and user behaviour, which can then be used for commercial gain. This is why it is important for libraries to be clear if third-party cookies are being used, and if they are, for library users to be able to fully understand their implications.

Table 8.1 *Types of cookie*

First-party cookie	Third-party cookie
Browser cookies, also known as HTTP cookies, web cookies or internet cookies. • They are essential to making the internet work. • They allow sites to identify you each time you visit them. • They store information about your previous activity on the site, the pages you have read, and username and password information. This type of cookie is not blocked by anti-spyware software.	Tracker cookies are a type of persistent cookie. • They are not necessary to make the internet work. • They are used by advertisers and third parties to monitor and track your online activity. • They are used to target specific adverts at you, based on what you have looked at online. • Any personal data gathered by them can be sold to other companies.
Non-persistent cookies	**Persistent cookies**
Non-persistent cookies, otherwise known as temporary cookies, are stored in RAM on the client's device and are destroyed when the browser is closed. They are only active for as long as the browser remains active. They are also called session cookies.	These are cookies which are virtually irrevocable (unkillable). **Evercookies** are a type of persistent cookie which is produced by a javascript API. Their goal is to identify a client even after they have removed the standard cookies. A **flash cookie**, or locally shared object, is a collection of cookie-like data that a website running Adobe Flash can place on your hard drive. They aren't easy to remove. However, browser settings and browser add-ons can be used to limit the duration of storage.

8.4 How is personal data being used by the library?

A privacy policy notice should make clear the purpose for which you are processing the personal data of library users. A typical personal data policy might read as follows:

> The purposes for which the Library may process your personal data include:

- the management of library accounts (including the issuing of library cards and the issuing, return and recall of loans)
- ensuring the security of our collections and the safety of our users through CCTV and turnstile swipe card data
- personalisation of services which might be of particular use to you - for example, disability, support, advice and request services
- our promotional and marketing initiatives, which you can also opt into, where we can proactively keep you informed of any service changes or projects.

We may use some of the information you provide us with for other reasons, including:

- to help us plan services for your future
- to make sure that the service you receive is efficient and effective
- to account for our decisions and investigate complaints
- to meet our statutory obligations
- to identify and protect those at risk of harm
- to ensure the accuracy of our records
- to prevent and detect crime
- to protect you and other people.

8.5   The purpose of a library privacy policy

A library privacy policy fulfils three purposes:

1 Internal - defines privacy practices within the library and as relates to the organisation
2 External - conveys privacy practices to patrons, law enforcement and others
3 Legal - protects against potential liability and public relations problems.

(Wise, 2015)

There isn't a one-size-fits-all library privacy policy statement which will be applicable for every library's circumstances. Libraries are instead expected to tailor their privacy policy notice to meet their own operational needs - ensuring that any elements specific to their own institution are covered.

8.6   RFID privacy policy

Book Industry Communication (BIC) has a template for an RFID (radio frequency identification) privacy policy at www.bic.org.uk/161/RFID-Privacy-in-Libraries. The policy has the following headings:

- Introduction
- What is RFID?
- What is the risk to privacy?
  - identifying the book
  - tracking the library book borrower.
- What steps have been taken to alert library users to the risk?
- Can the risk be reduced?
- What should a member of the public do?
- Conclusion.

8.7   Privacy policies and public access terminals in libraries

In September 2009 there was a discussion thread on the JISCMail data protection list relating to public access terminals in libraries. When a library user wanted to access the internet in his local library he was asked either to enter his local 'smartcard' details or his library card data.

This raises a number of privacy issues for him, and yet none of these seemed to be addressed at the pre-login screen. The library user wondered: Is what I do on these access points recorded? If so, for what purpose? And, is it recorded against my personal details? As a result, he resorted to asking his local council for comments.

8.8   Examples of library privacy policy notices

For a few examples of privacy policy notices which have been written specifically for national, university and public libraries see the following:

British Library privacy notice: www.bl.uk/aboutus/terms/privacy.
Croydon council library privacy notice:
www.croydon.gov.uk/democracy/data-protection-freedom-information/
privacy-notices/library-services-privacy-notice.
University of Gloucestershire library service privacy notice:
www.glos.ac.uk/docs/download/Privacy-notices/GDPR-Privacy
%20Notice-Library-Service.pdf.
University of West London library services privacy notice:
www.uwl.ac.uk/library/about-library/policies-and-regulations/
library-services-privacy-notice-library-visitors.

According to Givens (2015), there are several library privacy policies that can serve as inspiration for libraries creating or updating their own privacy policies. Each library's policy should address the library's unique privacy issues. Individuals creating library privacy policies should examine the library's information privacy practices and these should be reflected in the privacy policy notice.

8.9 Third-party access

There are three reasons why third-party access is a matter of concern:

1 The problem lies in the data collection policies of third parties. If those companies were to fail, what would happen to the data they have collected? Many times, the only asset a failing business has is the data it had collected, which could lead it to sell the data to anyone, including insurance companies (Cyrus and Baggett, 2012).
2 What happens to data held by third-party services when you end your relationship with the primary provider? (Edwards, 2016).
3 It's worth stating: if you don't control your infrastructure and your path to customers, your entire business is at the mercy of a third party (Carpenter, 2016).

The library's privacy policy statement should cover: the recipients or categories of recipient you disclose the personal data to and why; and what those recipients will do with the data. It might look like this:

Your personal data will be forwarded to the following third parties in connection with services provided by the Library:
XYZ company will retain information for the purposes of accepting payments for library charges.
Other external organisations to enable us to provide library services to you:
- SirsiDynix Symphony (Library Management System)
- Bolinda (Borrow Box)
- RB Digital (E-Zines, E-Audio, E-Books)
- Bibliotheca (Self-Service Machines)
(etc.)

The personal data that you have provided will not routinely be sent to other third-parties (unless notified).

8.10 Payment card details

If your library processes payments made with credit or debit cards, the privacy policy statement should include a brief note about the processing of payment card data. For example:

Where credit/debit card details have been requested as part of a transaction between you and us, these details will be encrypted and handled by a secure web server using SSL technology.
If you make a payment by credit/debit card the library uses a secure

third-party service from XYZ company.

Certain information you provide will automatically be recorded by XYZ company. See www.xyzcompany.com/privacy for further details.

8.11   How are privacy policies communicated to users?

Libraries need to think about how best to convey information about privacy to their users. Being open and transparent about the personal data that is being collected, how it is used, whether it is shared, and how it is kept secure is essential to building a relationship of trust with library users. Is there anything about privacy in the library which is clearly visible to library users? What message does it convey? Will it catch the eye of library users? If a member of the public walked into your library, how easy would it be for them to find any information about the way in which you handle the personal data of library users?

⟿ Opportunities for libraries to convey a message about privacy to its users

There are a number of different opportunities for libraries to communicate a privacy message to its users. These include:

- Written policy with library card issuance
- Notices, posters and signs
- On the library website
- Correspondence with users on renewal of library membership for a further year
- Privacy awareness or online safety training session.

One example would be to have the BIC RFID privacy poster displayed prominently on library premises. This consists of the RFID symbol being prominently displayed, accompanied by the words 'RFID is in use on these premises', with details of where users can find out more and inspect the library's privacy policy. It shows the URL of where to find the privacy policy. A similar message, such as that in Figure 8.1 on the next page, should be used to inform library users where CCTV is in operation.

It is important to take account of the needs of all library users. For example, you might want to have a copy of the privacy note printed in large text so that this can be given to any library users who are unable to use the library computers or who have sight difficulties.

**CCTV is in use on
these premises**
www.nowheresville.gov.uk/privacy/cctv/

Figure 8.1 *Example of a CCTV use notice*

Signs should:

- be clearly visible and readable
- contain details of the organisation operating the system, the purpose for using the surveillance system and who to contact about the scheme (where these things are not obvious to those being monitored)
- include basic contact details, such as a simple website address and telephone number or e-mail contact
- be an appropriate size depending on context (Information Commissioner's Office, 2017a).

CHAPTER 9

Data protection and privacy audits

Data protection and privacy audits consist of a review and evaluation of the institution's data protection and privacy policies and procedures. The audit should establish how personal data is being processed, and whether the institution's privacy policy statement and other relevant documentation reflects this. Is it doing what it says it does?

There are four things that an audit team should do to help minimise risk:

1 Review processes used to collect, analyse, store and share personal information.
2 Ensure the appropriate controls are incorporated into all projects.
3 Test the effectiveness of privacy training and awareness initiatives.
4 Make improvements as appropriate in library staff awareness and behaviours relating to privacy risks.

Library staff training and awareness initiatives should be tested in order to assess whether or not they have led to staff being more privacy-aware. Is the training sufficiently practical in nature? Does it enable library staff to translate privacy concepts into their day-to-day responsibilities?

9.1   Why carry out a data protection audit?

The main reasons for carrying out data protection audits are:

- to assess the level of compliance with data protection legislation (GDPR, DPA 2018, PECR)
- to assess the level of compliance with the institution's own data protection system
- to identify potential gaps and weaknesses in the data protection system
- to provide information for review and improvement of the data protection system.

Data protection audits should be conducted regularly and should reflect any changes in the law. They should help to reduce the likelihood of data breaches occurring where these are caused by poor procedures and insufficient or ineffective training programmes.

9.2   Know your data

The starting point should be to audit the types of personal data that the library processes and the devices (including their ownership) used to hold it.

- Certify that all personal information stored by the library has been classified, inventoried, and had its location mapped.
- Verify that each data type has a clear owner responsible for monitoring access and for approving any requests to share the data with third parties.

9.2.1   Sensitive personal data

An important step to take when you address the question 'What personal data do you collect' is to identify which of this data constitutes sensitive personal data (see Figure 1.1, p. 4). Once you have inventoried the types of sensitive personal data that you collect, ask yourself:

- When library staff access sensitive personal data is their activity tracked or audited?
- Is there a focus on the sensitive personal data found in unstructured data such as e-mails and documents?

9.3   Deletion of data

One aspect of the audit should look at the destruction of data:

- Verify that data collected by the library is destroyed when no longer necessary.
- Check that records are automatically destroyed in accordance with the records retention schedule.
- Review data destruction methods to confirm that they result in the permanent destruction of information.

9.3.1   Hidden data

There are many potential data caches. Even if you delete data, it could potentially be recreated from:

- log files
- backups
- metadata
- caches and mirrors
- proxies
- upstream storage and ISPs
- partners, suppliers, vendors, third-party services.

9.4   Conducting a library privacy audit

9.4.1   Preparing for the audit

Identify all of the systems that are used to process data (Table 9.1) For each of them, ask the questions in Table 9.2 and map the answers against what constitutes fair processing.

Table 9.1 *Library systems to be audited*

System types	Systems	Examples
Library application systems	Patron database (current and former users) Borrowing history records Fines and payment history Document delivery Reservation requests Interlibrary loan requests Electronic reserves Online catalogue/library account logs Saved searches Citations lists/bibliographies Automated search profiles (SDI) 'My library' personalisations	Example: Database backups and server logs Can deleted data be recreated from log files, backups, caches, proxies and mirrors? Example: Saved citation lists or bibliographies Encourage users to delete lists they are no longer using Remove lists associated with inactive accounts
Websites and servers	Web server logs Proxy server logs Forms and e-mail Website analytics	Example: Web logs If using web logs for statistical analysis, gather the data immediately and then purge the logs If logs must be kept, anonymise the data
Public computers	Browser history and cache Cookies Files used/saved by library users Information from online forms saved on PC Computer booking system usage logs Website log-ins saved on public computers	Example: Data saved on public computers (such as website log-ins, files saved by library users) Use software to automatically return library PCs to their native state when a user has finished with the machine

Continued

Table 9.1 *Continued*

System types	Systems	Examples
Remote services	Log-ins (in library or from home) Personalisation Statistics Mobile devices Wi-Fi usage logs	Example: BYOD mobile devices Do systems accessed through mobile devices have appropriate controls to limit data access and detect malicious activity?
Other	CCTV logs Attendees lists and personal registration details for events Printing history	Example: CCTV Access to information such as CCTV logs or the stored images should be restricted Clear signage to inform patrons that CCTV is in use

Table 9.2 *Questions to ask regarding each system processing personal data*

Questions to ask	Measure the answers against these rules for data collection
What data is being collected?	Only collect the information needed for the task in question: the data minimisation principle
Where is it located?	Ensure that if you transfer personal data to a non-EEA processor, that you are able to do so in compliance with the GDPR
Who has access?	Measures to ensure data security – access should be limited to only those people who must work with the data (least-privilege model)
How long is the data kept?	Limited storage periods – is the data kept only for as long as it is needed to perform the function?
How is the data protected?	Appropriate technical and organisational measures

9.4.2   The audit process

The process follows a five-step lifecycle, as illustrated in Figure 9.1.

Step 1	Audit planning
Step 2	Audit preparation
Step 3	Conduct of the compliance audit
Step 4	Compliance audit reporting
Step 5	Audit follow-up review

Figure 9.1 *The data protection audit lifecycle*

Step 1: Audit planning

The more work that is put in to the planning and preparation of an audit, the smoother the conduct of the audit will be on the day. The five key aspects of audit planning are these:

1 Carry out a risk assessment:
   - Break the institution down into distinct areas, capable of being audited as distinct entities. Typically, these will correspond to departments, functions or processes. A basic risk assessment must be carried out for each one. The results will be used to determine audit priorities and help judge how frequently each area needs to be audited.
   - Review the processes used to identify, monitor and manage threats and vulnerabilities. Review the frequency of risk assessments, and evaluate the comprehensiveness of inputs into the process.
2 Draw up an internal audit schedule.
3 Select a suitable auditor.
4 Send off the pre-audit questionnaire.
5 The auditor holds a preparatory meeting.

See also the checklist at the end of this chapter.

Step 2: Audit preparation

This covers the activities undertaken by the auditor immediately after the preparatory meeting until the audit itself.

An adequacy audit should be conducted, with the following two purposes:

1 to assess the extent to which the organisation's data protection system meets the requirements of the Data Protection Act 2018, GDPR and PECR
2 to determine whether it will be beneficial to conduct a compliance audit or to delay matters until issues identified in the adequacy audit have been addressed.

It is possible that the adequacy audit may conclude that the organisation has very little data protection documentation in place, that its procedures are inadequate, and that there is insufficient data protection awareness training. If the auditor uncovers major deficiencies at the preliminary stage, the organisation must decide how to proceed:

- The organisation may go ahead with the compliance audit to help formulate potential solutions to address weaknesses identified.

- The auditor could say that it is pointless to conduct the compliance audit until the major deficiencies have been addressed.
- The auditor could refer the organisation to the Information Commissioner to rectify their data protection system's deficiencies.

Step 3: Conduct of the compliance audit

The purpose of the opening meeting is for the auditor to meet senior library staff with responsibility for data protection and ensure they understand what the auditor is planning to do by running through:

- the scope of the audit
- the audit plan
- meetings with staff
- staff affected
- reporting findings
- follow-up
- practical arrangements.

A **functional audit** involves checking the operation of the data protection system within a specific area, function or department. A **process audit** involves auditing a particular process from beginning to end where it has data protection implications. It may cut across different areas, functions or departments. The auditor needs to visit all locations where the process takes place. He or she will need to question directly library staff who carry out the tasks, and must avoid letting others answer the questions on their behalf. **Staff interviews** are used to assess staff awareness of data protection issues, particularly where staff routinely handle personal data. They are best achieved through one-to-one interviews or via small focus groups.

Step 4: Compliance audit reporting

Data protection audit results must be formally documented and presented to the organisation at the end of the audit. This provides the organisation with valuable information regarding the status of its data protection system, and specifically:

- a formal record of which areas of the organisation were audited and when
- an indication of areas which appear to comply with the requirements of the GDPR, PECR and DPA
- details of areas that do not appear to comply with the GDPR, PECR and DPA, along with reasons for each non-compliance and the associated significance/risk
- a suggested programme of corrective action, along with target dates.

Step 5: Audit follow-up/review

If any instances of non-compliance are discovered during the audit, it is desirable to undertake a follow-up to check that the proposed corrective action has been implemented and has proved to be effective. The scope of follow-up action should be chosen according to the severity level of the initial non-compliance. It could take a number of different forms:

- telephone confirmation that minor adjustments have been made
- documentation checks
- re-audit of the area(s) where non-compliance(s) was initially identified
- re-audit of an entire area or department where a substantial lack of adequate controls or a systematic disregard of procedures was discovered.

The information will be recorded in the compliance audit report during the closing meeting.

The timescale of the follow-up action should be chosen according to the severity level of the original non-compliance and the original risk assessment of the data protection processing activities involved. Major non-compliances may require immediate corrective action, whereas it may be decided that minor non-compliances can be left until the next scheduled audit of the area or department.

⇢Data protection and privacy audit checklist

- When do we collect information?
- What information do we collect?
  - name
  - postal address
  - e-mail address
  - phone number
  - ID number
  - age/date of birth
  - ethnicity
  - marital status
  - gender
  - financial information
  - IP address
- Why is the information collected?
- Who collects this information?
- Who has access to the information?
- Who else processes the data?
- Who stores the data and how is it stored?
- Where is this information kept?

- How long is it held for?
- How is the information used?
- Who protects the data and how is it made secure?
- How and when is the information destroyed?
- Who 'owns' the data?
- How would compromise of this data impact the library?
- How would compromise of this data impact library patrons?

CHAPTER 10

Data protection impact assessments

Data protection impact assessments (DPIA) are a tool which can help organisations identify the most effective way to comply with their data protection obligations and meet library users' expectations of privacy.

DPIAs are covered in Article 35 and Recital 84 of the GDPR. They are used by organisations to identify, understand and address data protection issues that might arise when they are developing new products and services or undertaking new activities involving the processing of personal data. Where processing operations are likely to result in a high risk to the rights and freedoms of natural persons, the GDPR requires the data controller to carry out a DPIA to evaluate the origin, nature, particularity and severity of that risk, taking into account the nature, scope, context and purposes of the processing and the sources of the risk. The outcome of the assessment should be taken into account when determining the appropriate measures required to demonstrate that the processing of personal data complies with the GDPR. Where a DPIA indicates that processing operations involve a high risk which the controller cannot mitigate by appropriate measures in terms of available technology and implementation costs, they should consult the Information Commissioner's Office *prior* to the processing taking place (see GDPR recital 84).

DPIAs are applied to new projects. This allows greater scope for influencing how the project will be implemented. They are also used when an organisation is planning changes to an existing service or procedure. An effective DPIA allows organisations to identify and fix problems in the early stages. They are an integral part of the privacy by design approach (see Article 25 of the GDPR), thereby reducing the associated costs and reputational damage that might otherwise occur.

The ICO's support materials covering DPIAs include: a web page containing guidance on DPIAs (Information Commissioner's Office, 2018a) and a draft DPIA template (Information Commissioner's Office, 2018b); the first of these has a number of links to more detailed guidance. The ICO's documentation is a useful starting point for developing a methodology which fits with the library's own needs and working practices. There is also an ICO code of practice (Information Commissioner's Office, 2014a) which provides useful guidance. It was, however, written at a time when privacy impact assessments (PIA) were merely seen as an example of best practice, whereas the GDPR sets out the circumstances where a DPIA should be carried out as a legal requirement.

⏵Useful resource – sample DPIA template

In 2018 the ICO issued a sample DPIA template
https://ico.org.uk/media/about-the-ico/consultations/2258461/dpia-template-
v04-post-comms-review-20180308.pdf.
This template is an example of how you can record your DPIA process and
outcome. It follows the process set out in the ICO's DPIA guidance, and it
should be read alongside that guidance and the criteria for an acceptable
DPIA set out in European guidelines on DPIAs (Article 29 Data Protection
Working Party, 2017).

Conducting a DPIA should benefit organisations by producing better policies
and systems. It involves working with people within the institution, with partner
organisations and with the people affected to identify and reduce privacy risks.
As such it should improve the relationship between the institution and its library
staff and between the institution and library users. Figure 10.1 sets out the stages
of a data protection impact assessment.

Step 1 – Identify the need for a DPIA
Step 2 – Describe the processing
Step 3 – Consultation process with stakeholders (internal/external)
Step 4 – Assess necessity and proportionality
Step 5 – Identify and assess risks
Step 6 – Identify measures to reduce risk
Step 7 – Sign off and record DPIA outcomes

Figure 10.1 *Stages of a data protection impact assessment*

10.1 What the data protection impact assessment must contain

GDPR Article 35, paragraph 7 says that a data protection impact assessment
must contain:

- a systematic description of the envisaged processing operations and the
  purposes of the processing, including, where applicable, the legitimate
  interest pursued by the controller
- an assessment of the necessity and proportionality of the processing
  operations in relation to the purposes
- an assessment of the risks to the rights and freedoms of data subjects
- the measures envisaged to address the risks, including safeguards, security
  measures and mechanisms to ensure the protection of personal data and to
  demonstrate compliance with the GDPR taking into account the rights and
  legitimate interests of data subjects and other persons concerned.

Compliance with approved codes of conduct[1] by data controllers or data processors is taken into due account when an assessment is made of the impact of the processing operations that they perform, in particular for the purposes of a data protection impact assessment.

10.2   Impact on privacy

A data protection impact assessment is focused on *informational privacy* – the ability of a person to control, edit, manage and delete information about themselves and to decide how and to what extent that information is communicated to others. Intrusions of informational privacy could be in the form of collecting an excessive amount of personal information, disclosing information without consent or misuse of that information. It would also cover the monitoring of the websites someone has visited.

Another privacy dimension is *physical privacy* – the ability of a person to maintain their own physical space or solitude. Intrusions of someone's physical privacy could take the form of unwelcome searches of their personal possessions such as: body searches by library security staff; acts of surveillance or the taking of biometric information, such as where school libraries require children to use their fingerprints to borrow books.

A project which has been subject to a DPIA should be less privacy-intrusive and therefore less likely to affect individuals in a negative way.

Conducting and publicising a DPIA provides libraries with an opportunity to build trust with their users. The actions they take during and after the DPIA process can improve the library's understanding of its users and their privacy concerns.

10.3   Steps involved in a data protection impact assessment
Step 1: Identify the need for a DPIA

The first stage of a DPIA is to identify whether or not such an assessment is needed. GDPR requires DPIAs to be undertaken where:

- a systematic evaluation of personal data results in legal effects to the data subject or affects them significantly
- there is large-scale processing of sensitive personal data or criminal convictions and offences data
- there is a large-scale systematic monitoring of a publicly accessible area.

For the precise form of words used in the legislation, see GDPR Article 35 (3). In order to establish whether a DPIA is needed, the ICO has a series of screening questions to identify the potential privacy impacts of the proposed new product/service:

- Will the project involve the collection of new information about individuals?
- Will the project compel individuals to provide information about themselves?
- Will information about individuals be disclosed to organisations or people who have not previously had routine access to the information?
- Are you using information about individuals for a purpose it is not currently used for, or in a way it is not currently used?
- Does the project involve you using new technology which might be perceived as being privacy-intrusive (for example, the use of biometrics or facial recognition)?
- Will the project result in you making decisions or taking action against individuals in ways which can have a significant impact on them?
- Is the information about individuals of a kind particularly likely to raise privacy concerns or expectations (for example, health records, criminal records or other information that people would consider to be particularly private)?
- Will the project require you to contact individuals in ways which they may find intrusive?

Source: *ICO Code of Practice* (Information Commissioner's Office, 2014a).

Step 2: Describe the processing

Its **nature** – what is the nature of the data? Does it include sensitive personal data or criminal convictions and offences data? Are children or vulnerable groups affected? How will the data be collected, used, stored and deleted? What is the source of the data? Will it be shared with anyone? What types of potentially high-risk processing have been identified?

Its **scope** – how much data? How long is it to be kept? How many individuals are affected? What geographical area does it cover?

Its **context** – what is the nature of your relationship with the affected individuals? How much control will they have? Would they expect you to use their data in this way? Are there prior concerns over this type of processing? Are there any known security flaws? Is it in any way novel? What is the current state of technology in this field? Are there any issues of current public concern that you should factor in? Are you signed up to an approved code of conduct?

Its **purpose** – what is the project intended to achieve? What is the intended effect on individuals? What are the benefits of the processing?

Step 3: Consultation process with stakeholders (internal/external)

It is important to discuss the privacy issues with stakeholders right from the start and throughout the DPIA process. There can be both internal and external stakeholders to consult, as listed in Table 10.1.

Table 10.1 *Types of stakeholders in a DPIA consultation*

Internal stakeholders	External stakeholders
Project management team	The affected individuals
Data protection officer	Vendors
Developers and designers	Cloud provider
Information technology	Partners
Procurement	
Potential suppliers and data processors	
Staff who will have to use the new system	
Senior management	

The library may already have a number of consultation mechanisms in place which can be utilised to gain a better understanding of library users' privacy expectations and experiences. These mechanisms could include focus groups, library user groups, public meetings and reading groups.

Step 4: Assess necessity and proportionality

The DPIA process requires an organisation to consider whether the project's impact on privacy is proportionate to the outcomes which will be achieved. Public bodies subject to the Human Rights Act 1998 can use the assessment to check that any of its actions which interfere with the right to private life, family life, home or correspondence (ECHR Article 8) are necessary and proportionate.

Ultimately, you need to consider whether the final impact on individuals after implementing each solution to mitigate the privacy risks represents a justified, compliant and proportionate response to the aims of the project.

Step 5: Identify and assess risks

Privacy risks are posed by data which is:

- inaccurate, insufficient or out of date
- excessive or irrelevant
- kept for too long
- disclosed to people who should not have access to it
- used in ways unacceptable to or unexpected by the data subject
- not kept securely.

The potential risks can be identified in terms of:

- potential for damage and distress to individuals
- financial and reputational risk to the institution from a data breach.

When identifying and assessing privacy risks:

- Record the risks to individuals, including possible intrusions on privacy where appropriate.
- Assess the institutional risks, including regulatory action, reputational damage, and loss of public trust.
- Conduct a compliance check against the DPA, GDPR, PECR and other relevant legislation.
- Maintain a record of the risks identified.

Privacy risks can lead to privacy harms, some of which are easier to quantify than others. The consequences of a data breach can include:

- losing (or being overlooked for) a job
- financial loss
- damage to personal relationships
- damage to social standing
- fear of identity theft (where data has been compromised, but where you aren't sure if it will be misused).

Some harms may seem inconsequential if you were to take them in isolation, but they could be extremely serious if the cumulative impact on society were to be fully taken into account. They could result in the loss of personal autonomy or dignity or they might exacerbate fears of excessive surveillance.

When Richard Thomas was the UK's Information Commissioner he warned that Britain could be sleepwalking into an East German-style surveillance society (Booth, 2004). Privacy, especially online privacy, is being lost a bit at a time, thereby making it harder to identify the precise point at which a line has been crossed. An analogy sometimes used is that of a boiling frog. This relates to an experiment where a frog is placed in a saucepan full of cold water. As the water is brought to the boil, the frog is oblivious to the danger. In the analogy, the frog only realises its predicament when it is too late, when they are unable to react and it ends up boiling to death. In other words, there is a real danger that people will only wake up to their loss of privacy when it is too late to do anything about it.

Step 6: Identify measures to reduce risk

For any risks that are identified, it is necessary to consider whether or not they can be eliminated, reduced or simply accepted. In order to identify and evaluate privacy solutions:

- devise ways to reduce or eliminate privacy risks
- assess the costs and benefits of each approach, looking at the privacy impact and the effect on project outcomes
- refer back to the privacy risk register until satisfied with the overall privacy impact.

Some of the more likely measures to reduce privacy risk include:

- opting not to collect or store particular types of information (data minimisation)
- keeping information only as long as necessary and planning for its secure destruction (limited storage periods)
- implementing appropriate technological security measures such as encryption
- ensuring library staff are properly trained and aware of potential privacy risks
- anonymisation or pseudonymisation of information where possible
- ensuring individual library users are fully aware of how their information is used and can contact the library for assistance if necessary (fairness and transparency)
- producing guidance for library staff on how to use new systems
- using systems which make it easy for individuals to access their information.

Step 7 – Sign off and record DPIA outcomes

When the DPIA has been completed, carry out the following tasks:

- obtain appropriate sign-off within the organisation
- produce a report drawing on material produced earlier in the DPIA process
- consider publishing the report or other relevant information about the process
- integrate the final outcomes of the DPIA back into the project plan
- ensure that the steps recommended by the DPIA are implemented.

10.4   Examples of where DPIAs would be used in libraries

A DPIA is appropriate for a number of library-related situations:

- selecting a new library management system

- selecting a discovery service
- replacing RFID self-service kiosks
- joining a library consortium where this involves data sharing
- entering into a shared IT project where library user data will be linked or pooled
- using existing data for a new purpose, such as feeding it into a learning analytics system.

Tables 10.2 on planning a new library management system and 10.3 on the installation of RFID self-service kiosks are intended to point out *some* of the things to consider when new projects are being planned that have the potential to impact upon the privacy of library users. They should only be seen as a starting point, rather than as a comprehensive list of all of the privacy issues to consider and how any risks can be mitigated.

Table 10.2 *DPIA for a project to install a new library management system*

Stage	What it covers	Applied to the introduction of a new library management system
1	What does the project aim to achieve and what type of processing does it involve?	The purpose of the LMS is to manage the daily operations of the library efficiently. The system manages the library catalogue and keeps a record of material borrowed.
2	Describe the nature of the processing (how the data will be collected, used, stored and deleted; the data source; any sharing of data).	Personal information will be collected when a user completes a library registration form in order to register for a library card. The form includes a privacy policy statement. The data will be used to manage circulation records, to chase up overdue items, and to record details of any fines that are due. Where users have outstanding debts (from overdue charges, from interlibrary loan requests, or from charges incurred for lost or damaged items), their details may be passed to a debt collection company solely for the purposes of recovering the outstanding debt. A list of valid user IDs will be provided to a number of online content providers for authentication purposes. The data is shared with the following third parties: • the library management system vendor, once this has been selected

Continued

Table 10.2 *Continued*

Stage	What it covers	Applied to the introduction of a new library management system
		• Bolinda (Borrow Box) • RB Digital (e-zines, e-audio, e-books) • Bibliotheca (Self-service machines) • Lorensberg (Netloan booking system for public access computers) etc.
2	The scope of the processing. The nature of the data, and whether it includes special-category data. How much data, how long is it to be kept, how many individuals affected.	The types of personal information about individuals collected in the system include name, telephone number, date of birth, home address, e-mail address and credit card number. The library website uses cookies: • to remember that the user has closed the 'This site uses cookies . . .' message • to track page usage and visitor profiles, the results of which are used to inform future development of the website. None of these cookies tracks browsing behaviour beyond the library website, nor do they gather personal information.
2	Describe the context of the processing: What is the nature of your relationship with the individuals? How much control will they have? Would they expect you to use their data in this way? Are children or vulnerable groups included? Are there prior concerns over this type of processing or any known security flaws? Is it novel in any way? What is the current state of technology in this area?	An individual can object to the specific uses of their personally identifiable information (PII), but this will result in them being unable to borrow library materials or to access the online resources.

Continued

Table 10.2 *Continued*

Stage	What it covers	Applied to the introduction of a new library management system
	Are there any issues of public concern you should factor in? Are you signed up to any approved code of conduct or certification scheme?	
2	Describe the purposes of the processing: What do you want to achieve? What is the intended effect on individuals? What are the benefits of the processing?	The data collected is required to enable patrons to obtain a library card so that they can borrow materials or access online resources. The new library management system will allow the library to introduce new services that users can opt into, including: • marketing software which will permit library users to receive e-mail notifications of new stock or library events that appeal to them or their families • interactive services, enabling users to post recommendations and reviews • a social platform for library communities, enabling users to connect with people with similar interests.
3	Consider how to consult relevant stakeholders.	Stakeholders to be consulted will include: • library users • library staff who will be briefed on the project plans • library volunteers • library partners. The LMS vendor will be required to answer a number of data protection and information security questions as part of the tendering process.
4	Describe compliance and proportionality measures.	The impact on privacy, once the risk mitigation measures have been implemented (use of HTTP secure (https://), encryption, and anonymisation of personally identifiable information after one year) is limited and proportionate.

Continued

Table 10.2 *Continued*

Stage	What it covers	Applied to the introduction of a new library management system
5	Describe the source of risk and nature of potential impact on individuals.	The privacy risks associated with the collection of PII are: • unauthorised access, • inaccurate information in the system, and • unauthorised disclosure of PII. There are technical, administrative and physical security measures in place to mitigate these risks.

Table 10.3 *DPIA for a project to install new RFID equipment*

Stage	What it covers	Applied to the installation of new RFID equipment
1	What does the project aim to achieve and what type of processing does it involve?	To install self-service kiosks. To use radio frequency identification tags in library books. Enables library users to self-issue and self-return library books.
2	Describe the nature of the processing (how the data will be collected, used stored and deleted; the data source; any sharing of data).	An RFID scanner at the self-service terminals will read the information on the tag which is placed inside each item of stock.
2	The scope of the processing. The nature of the data, and whether it includes special-category data. How much data, how long is it to be kept, how many individuals affected.	No personal data will be stored on the tags (a review of the RFID tags deployed on books will be undertaken to ensure that this is the case).
2	Describe the context of the processing: What is the nature of your relationship with the individuals? How much control will they have?	Codes and standards we work to include: • BIC RFID Code of Practice • BIC RFID privacy poster • EU mandate M/436 and standards 16570 and 16571.

Continued

Table 10.3 *Continued*

Stage	What it covers	Applied to the installation of new RFID equipment
2	Would they expect you to use their data in this way? Do they include children or other vulnerable groups? Are there prior concerns over this type of processing or security flaws? Is it novel in any way? What is the current state of technology in this area? Are there any issues of public concern you should factor in? Are you signed up to any approved code of conduct or certification scheme?	The current state of the technology recognises the need to comply with the requirements of the GDPR, and the RFID systems vendors are also mindful of EU Mandate M/436 on Privacy in RFID (and the standards EN 16570 and EN 16571 which are designed to implement Mandate M/436's recommendations), even though the Mandate isn't currently in force. BIC works with the RFID vendors, as do a number of individual library authorities, on measures that could be taken to mitigate the RFID risk to privacy. They work on an ongoing basis to identify potential privacy solutions which can be applied to existing deployments, as well as towards future technological innovations. The GDPR's privacy by design and by default means that vendors should now have privacy as a cornerstone of any future technologies.
2	Describe the purposes of the processing: What do you want to achieve? What is the intended effect on individuals? What are the benefits of the processing for you, and more broadly?	The anticipated benefits include: • the need for less staff intervention, • convenience for library users, and • giving users greater control and independence • enabling the library to operate issue and return processes through self-service kiosks • improving stock management • improving security.
3	Consider how to consult relevant stakeholders.	At the planning stage for the project to install RFID, the library involves relevant stakeholders: • library staff • volunteers • library users • the systems vendor • stock suppliers in process. Site visits are undertaken to neighbouring authorities who have RFID installed in order to learn best practice.

Continued

Table 10.3 *Continued*

Stage	What it covers	Applied to the installation of new RFID equipment
3		Once the equipment has been installed, a number of measures will be implemented to ensure that library patrons are fully informed of the use of RFID technology and its privacy implications: • Notices and other signage are displayed prominently in the library to inform library visitors and borrowers of the use of RFID. • BIC RFID posters are displayed next to the self-service kiosks. • The RFID notification logo is visible wherever RFID is in use on the library premises. • The local authority has developed an RFID privacy policy to explain to users what the library is doing to protect their privacy. • Both the Code of Practice and the RFID Privacy Policy are available on the premises and online for reference by visitors, borrowers, management and staff. • The library corresponds with users when they are issued with their library card or renew their library membership for another year. A note is included about the slight privacy risk. • A member of library staff with the designated role of 'privacy officer' is always available within a reasonable timescale to deal with any enquiries about the library privacy policy, including the RFID privacy policy.
4	Describe compliance and proportionality measures.	To read UK tags (VHF) the reader needs to be in very close proximity.
5	Describe the source of risk and nature of potential impact on individuals.	The privacy risks are small; nevertheless, most library users will be unaware of any risks and need to be informed so that they can make an informed choice as to whether or not to use the library and any precautions they should take to safeguard their privacy.

Continued

Table 10.3 *Continued*

Stage	What it covers	Applied to the installation of new RFID equipment
		Identified risks to privacy: • unauthorised reading of RFID tags • obtaining information about someone's identity, lifestyle, tastes, interests, sexual orientation or political affiliations • ability to track the user's movements. The risks exist because the tags are always on, available to be read so that library users can self-return items. In order to fully assess and mitigate the privacy risks a DPIA will be undertaken. Risks identified by the DPIA will be mitigated by the choice of RFID tags, the data that will be held on them, and the use of encryption.

Note

1   Article 40 of the GDPR permits associations and other bodies to prepare a code of conduct or amend an existing code which they then submit to the supervisory authority, which will indicate whether the code provides sufficient appropriate safeguards and complies with the GDPR.

CHAPTER 11

Privacy issues and vendors

Protecting the privacy of library users is far more complex than it once was. This can be attributed in part to the way in which library services are now delivered. Libraries rely heavily on technology and content providers in order to be able to deliver their services. The library is not simply a service provider. It is also a consumer of commercial products. That is true whether we are thinking of public libraries, academic libraries, school libraries, government libraries, commercial libraries or libraries in the third sector.

In addition, information management practices, cybersecurity protocols and legal frameworks all change over time. Given that libraries staunchly defend patron privacy and confidentiality, the question one needs to consider is: how successful have they been in carrying over those values and aspirations into a multi-vendor world?

It is essential to consider the security vulnerabilities in the library's supply chain. The risks posed by the following types of third-party relationships are huge: vendors; suppliers; partners.

11.1   Vendors and data breaches

A global survey of 347 corporate privacy professionals (Bloomberg Law and International Association of Privacy Professionals, 2016) identifies employees and vendors as two huge sources of risk that corporations are failing to manage properly. Examples of data breaches amongst vendors used by libraries include the following:

- Reed Elsevier - owner of LexisNexis - said that social security numbers, drivers' licence information and addresses of 310,000 people may have been stolen (Timmons, 2015).
- Bloomberg - in 2013 there were news stories to the effect that reporters at Bloomberg News had used a Bloomberg function that tracks how recently a client has logged in as a way of generating story leads about personnel changes (Chozick and Protess, 2013).
- Adobe - in the autumn of 2014 there were a number of reports that Adobe Digital Editions was sending back detailed data to the Adobe servers in plain (unencrypted) text. This included a list of books read.
- An OverDrive/Amazon tie-in led to accusations of their library lending

programme being 'anti-user, anti-intellectual freedom, anti-library' and of libraries having been 'screwed'. Concerns were expressed over the data about library users' borrowing practices being in the hands of a corporation (Kingsley-Hughes, 2011).

Ard (2013) notes that 'Because third parties like Amazon are not libraries, libraries' actor-defined confidentiality rules do not restrict them despite their involvement in library transactions and their collection of the very sorts of data the library confidentiality regime is meant to protect'.

Magi (2010) says that 'Librarians have a long history of protecting user privacy, but they have done seemingly little to understand or influence the privacy policies of library resource vendors that increasingly collect user information through Web 2.0-style personalisation features'.

Cox (2019) says that Elsevier left a server open to the public internet, exposing user e-mail addresses and passwords of people from universities and educational institutions across the world; and that the server was misconfigured due to human error.

11.2   Working with library vendors to maximise privacy

Do you work with vendors to ensure that professional values are baked in to the technology and platforms that are available on the market? According to Cowell (2016) 'Librarians need to own and debate these issues and demand vendors reflect our needs not theirs'.

Dixon (2006) claims that 'If libraries only chose vendors who had good privacy policies, the industry would have to change its standards in order to obtain library business'. That makes a lot of sense. However, Dixon's view does need to be put into perspective.

Buschman (2016, 424) says that the three largest publishers (Reed Elsevier, Pearson and Thomson Reuters) have less than 9% of the revenue of the three largest tech companies (Apple, Google and Microsoft). The biggest publishers' net income is about 5.5% that of the three top technologies, and their brand value is miniscule compared to that of the technology companies. In short, libraries represent only a sliver of the Reed/Pearson/Thomson markets, and the importance of privacy is proportionally diminished as a concern.

West (2016) identifies two main ways in which libraries could be doing a lot better in the realm of cybersecurity. First, to advocate for patron privacy. Second, to provide information about existing threat environments. She believes that part of this involves putting pressure on vendors – since libraries buy a lot of third-party software and tools – to provide safer tools and better practices. By way of example, West makes the point that 'we still have leading ILS vendors offering software that e-mails patrons a password in plain text. This has never been a best practice and has been a bad idea for multiple decades now. It is never necessary.'

How are vendors going to know what libraries want if we don't tell them? Library and information professionals need to take a lead on this; they need to work with vendors to ensure that the products offered to market are fit for purpose, and respectful of patron privacy. The key takeaway from this is that if we ask for changes, our vendors are responsive to working with us to ensure the security and privacy of patron data.

11.2.1 Points to consider before purchasing technology or content from external providers

- Libraries should make privacy a criterion when purchasing content.
- Vendors should disclose their policies and practices around user data.
- Licence agreements and contracts should address privacy issues.
- Libraries should inform users of the privacy implications when accessing online content.

11.2.2 Identifying security vulnerabilities in products you already have

Contact the vendors when you identify security vulnerabilities in their products. You may be surprised by how responsive they can be. They will want to improve their platforms, and will work towards having secure systems in place.

There are examples of libraries switching products on the basis of how respectful they are of privacy:

- Miami-Dade Public Library System switched from OverDrive to Axis 360 (Miami-Dade Public Library System, 2016).
- Cornell University Library switched from using Google Analytics to Piwik (now Matomo) (Chandler and Wallace, 2016).
- An academic library in the UK switched from their previous LMS supplier to using a combination of open-source products. This allowed them to retain control and ownership of their data.

And there are also examples of the vendors themselves taking action to be more protective of patron privacy:

- Summon and Primo removed Amazon trackers.
- Worldcat.org got rid of its ad trackers.

Do library vendors retain full control over library user data, so that if one uses their website it is impossible for third parties such as advertisers, social networks or analytics companies to violate patron privacy? Or does your vendor's privacy policy statement say something along these lines:

> We're not responsible for the privacy practices of websites operated by third parties linked to/integrated with our sites.

And how do the vendors enforce their privacy policy? Do they undertake regular privacy audits?

When library users establish which services are available to them through the library, how many of those people actually take the time to review the terms and conditions of the services that they use? They should bear in mind that these services are actually provided by commercial companies. One example of a service which is available through many public libraries – and indeed through other library types such as some corporate libraries – is PressReader. The service gives users access to thousands of newspapers and magazines from many different countries around the world in dozens of different languages. What possible downside could there be to using a service that offers such a wealth of resources? Only the most determined of users, one who checks what permissions they are giving the vendor when they download the app, will realise that they are allowing the vendor to read the contents of their USB storage as well as the ability to modify or delete the contents of their USB storage (source: https://play.google.com/store/apps/details?id=com.newspaperdirect.pressreader.android&hl=en_GB).

11.3   Vendor privacy policies

Lambert, Parker and Bashir (2015) undertook an analysis of the privacy policies of digital content vendors. They examined whether these privacy policies (1) meet the privacy standards of the library community, (2) meet other industry standards, and (3) are accessible and understandable to public library patrons. Their study found that the policies fail to meet the heightened standards of the library community.

One e-book platform's privacy policy says that they share information only with referring libraries, content providers, third-party service providers and security monitoring agents. Information collected by that e-book platform includes:

- recent titles accessed or borrowed
- personally identifiable information (including name, e-mail, password and communications preferences)
- payment settings (including credit card information)
- e-mail notification settings
- recommendations.

If the vendors that libraries use are collecting patron data, do we know enough about precisely why those vendors are collecting all of that information? If not, information professionals need to start asking questions, and to make sure that the questions they ask are sufficiently probing.

➡Library checklist for assessing vendors and suppliers

- What patron data will the vendor collect?
- How will the patron data be used?
- How will it be secured?
- Will it be shared with third parties?
- What are the contractual protections in the event of data breaches?
- What are the contractual requirements for data processors to notify the library of data breaches?
- What actions will be consequential on data breaches?
- Do you have an effective vendor management system in place where you can see if the vendor is doing their job correctly?
- Is there an indemnity clause covering third-party claims?

Think about the implications of outsourcing library functions, of using cloud providers or of using external contractors and consultants, and the agreements you have with them regarding the collecting, storing or processing of personal data. External contractors may include: data centres; payroll processors; external advisers; IT service providers; and cloud solutions.

11.3.1 Due diligence

The following list suggests some of the due diligence that should be performed on potential external contractors:

- Carry out pre-contractual checks of data processors seeking to be appointed by the library.
- Contractual conditions need to set out the library's requirements for the processing of personal data.
- Take up trade references.
- Subcontractors should also be subject to due diligence.

11.3.2 The ideal scenario

Agreements between libraries and vendors should specify:

- that libraries retain ownership of all data
- that the vendor agrees to observe the library's privacy, data retention and security policies

- that the vendor agrees to bind any third parties it uses in delivering services to these policies as well.

Other points to bear in mind when dealing with vendors on privacy issues are these:

- Know your vendor/service provider.
- Avoid clauses containing limitations of liability for breaches of confidential information. Remember: you can delegate responsibility but not accountability.
- Have a frank conversation with vendors about their data breach philosophy, and their information security measures.
- Get rid of data you don't need. Don't pass it on to vendors (data minimisation).
- If a data breach happens through a vendor make sure they will work with you to manage it.
- Draw up a data breach plan.
- Build a breach response team.
- Test the data breach response plan.
- How good are the vendor's internal privacy practices? What standards do they meet?

11.4   Measuring the cybersecurity of vendors

Carry out a cybersecurity risk management audit. Caro and Markman (2016) provide detail on how to do this (Table 11.1 opposite). Use a vendor security matrix to evaluate the security of each of your vendors (Table 11.2 on p. 152).

You can also use the following checklist (reproduced from Charillon (2018) under a CC0 public domain licence) to assess vendors and suppliers:

1 Does our library service have written contracts with all suppliers that process library users' personal information?
2 Have contracts and agreements with suppliers been updated to include GDPR requirements?
3 Has the supplier explained how its product and processes comply with GDPR?
4 Has the supplier communicated or discussed its data retention policy with the library service?
5 Do suppliers offering a service directly to library users have a clear, easy-to-find and easy-to-understand privacy statement?
6 Does the supplier use encryption (e.g. https for websites) to keep data secure?

7 Does the supplier use encryption by default for all processes - both when the data is in transit and when it is stored?

8 Does the supplier offer the option of opting out of personalisation features?

9 Has the supplier's system undergone a security audit? If so, are the results available? How were any gaps addressed?

10 Could your library service work with others (in a consortium or a national library organisation) to approach suppliers to ask for changes?

Table 11.1 *Cybersecurity risk management audit of library vendors (Reproduced from Caro and Markman (2016) under a Creative Commons Attribution 3.0 United States licence)*

Criteria	Brief description
1 Data breach policy	Is there a formal process in place to report data breaches if/when they occur?
2 Data encryption	If patron data is stored by the vendor, is it encrypted?
3 Data retention	Does the vendor purge patron search history records on a regular basis?
4 TOS 'Ease of use'	Can the average patron read and fully understand the vendor's terms of use policy?
5 Patron privacy	Does the vendor use Google Analytics or other tracking software to monitor users?
6 Secure connections	Does the vendor's website enforce secure connections only? (HTTPS or better?)
7 Advertising networks	Does the vendor's website participate in ad networks?

Table 11.2 *Vendor security matrix*

Criteria	Possible answers
http/https	http https
TLS	Is TLS used? Yes/No Which version of TLS?
Password	Plain text Plain text in URL Weak hash Strong token
User ID/e-mail	E-mail E-mail and ID E-mail and password Obfuscated
PII	Is PII exposed in URI? Yes/No Is it encrypted? Yes/No
Query parameters	Does it include: • device information? • user information?
Payload	JSON (JavaScript Object Notation) Text/html xhtml SOAP (Simple Object Access Protocol)

CHAPTER 12

Practical steps to protect the privacy of library users

Librarians may well wonder what they can do to protect patron privacy. Even where library and information professionals have a strong belief in the need to protect the privacy of their users, they may be at a loss to know what they can do to make any meaningful difference.

12.1 Twenty-six practical steps to protect your users' privacy

Below is a list of 26 practical steps that librarians can take to protect the privacy of their users. These include steps to protect privacy on public access terminals; education and training initiatives; information security measures; and vendor management. The brief checklist below is followed by a more detailed explanation for each step.

1 Use a search engine respectful of privacy.
2 Use a web browser respectful of privacy.
3 Use ad-blocking software.
4 Use software to return library PCs to their native state.
5 Organise a cryptoparty.
6 Develop a privacy discussion and knowledge-sharing forum.
7 Offer digital privacy training to your users.
8 Create an area on the library website dedicated to privacy issues.
9 Monitor security alerts and install software patches and updates to defend against attacks.
10 Use the full range of information security defences.
11 Undertake regular penetration testing to mitigate the risk of data security breaches.
12 Carry out a cybersecurity risk management audit of your vendors.
13 Use Transport Layer Security (TLS) on websites you host.
14 Ensure licence agreements contain robust privacy and confidentiality provisions.
15 Where data is housed in a vendor-controlled data centre, librarians should know where it is located, and what certifications the facility has.
16 Use https for your websites.

17 Safely wipe equipment before disposing of it.
18 Check if embedded content is leaking data to third parties.
19 Use a secure form of authentication.
20 Sign up to the Library Digital Privacy Pledge.
21 Use the NISO (2015) patron privacy framework.
22 Ensure that users can only retrieve printouts by swiping their library card.
23 Undertake a DPIA when introducing new services/making changes to existing ones.
24 Use browser add-ons to protect patron privacy.
25 Make sure any website analytics software you use is respectful of privacy.
26 Check the referrer http header policy on your websites.

Step 1

On public access terminals set the default search engine to one which respects privacy, such as:

Duckduckgo (https://duckduckgo.com)
Oscobo (www.oscobo.com)
Peekier (www.peekier.com)
Qwant (www.qwant.com)
Search Incognito (www.searchincognito.com)
Startpage (www.startpage.com)
SearX (https://searx.me), a metasearch engine which aggregates the results of other search engines.

Step 2

Use a browser that is respectful of privacy, and set it to be your default browser. Examples include:

Firefox (www.mozilla.org/en-GB/firefox/new)
Brave (https://brave.com)
Tor (short for The Onion Router) for anonymous browsing (www.torproject.org/projects/torbrowser.html.en).

Step 3

Use a browser extension to filter out advertisements. One of the reasons people choose to block adverts is to protect their privacy. Other reasons include protecting themselves against malware and having a better user experience. It is important to look in more detail at the ad blockers that are available and how they work, because they don't automatically block all advertisements. Adblock plus, for example, says that 'acceptable ads' are allowed by default (referring to advertisements which are considered not to be intrusive or annoying).

Adblock Plus (https://adblockplus.org)
Ghostery (www.ghostery.com).

Step 4

Use software to automatically return library PCs to their native state when a user has finished with the machine: www.raymond.cc/blog/reboot-windows-and-automatically-restore-to-its-original-state.

Clean Slate (www.fortresgrand.com/products/cls/cls.htm) software:

- protects computers from unwanted programs
- prevents files from being modified or deleted
- protects system configuration from changes
- protects the desktop look and feel from being changed.

Step 5

Organise a cryptoparty. These events are an opportunity to share with people the basics of cryptography, such as the use of the Tor browser, disk encryption, the use of virtual private networks, and secret messaging. Some libraries have organised cryptoparties jointly with organisations such as Scottish PEN (https://scottishpen.org) and Open Rights Group (www.openrightsgroup.org). Belveze (2017) has written an article about how librarians can contribute to students' and citizens' empowerment against tracking and mass surveillance by organising cryptoparties.

Step 6

Develop a forum to discuss privacy issues and share best practice and knowledge of tools. This could be a natural extension of a series of privacy training events or cryptoparties.

Step 7

Include privacy within any digital literacy training offered to your users. Masur, Teutsch and Trepte (2017) have developed an online privacy literacy scale (OPLIS) in which they have put together a number of questions covering knowledge about institutional practices, technical aspects of data protection, data protection law and data protection strategies.

Training should be tailored according to the type of audience. There will be a need to train library staff and library volunteers, as well as library users and local businesses.

Step 8

Create an area on the library website dedicated to privacy issues. There is a useful resource available from the San Jose Public Library (www.sjpl.org/privacy). Their site lets you generate a custom privacy toolkit geared towards your own organisation's online needs.

Step 9

In order to be better protected against new and evolving threats, install software patches and updates. This will help defend against attacks. Vulnerabilities are constantly being discovered, therefore it is imperative to have the latest updates. To make the job of updating software easier, make use of software updater tools to keep your software updated to the latest versions. Your internet security software may include such a feature.

Step 10

Use a full range of information security defences: firewall, intrusion detection system (IDS), intrusion protection system (IPS), web filtering, antivirus, etc.

Step 11

Undertake regular penetration testing (using ethical hackers) and network security checks to mitigate the risk of data security breaches. Do this for both internal and external systems.

Step 12

Carry out a cybersecurity risk management audit of your vendors (see the useful article by Caro and Markman (2016) and Table 11.1 in the previous chapter on the topic). Caro and Markman believe that internal audits should be conducted in order to ensure that content partners and IT vendors take cybersecurity as seriously as library staff do.

Step 13

Use Transport Layer Security (TLS) on websites you host. It is possible to test the TLS/SSL security of a website or browser using SSLLabs (www.ssllabs.com).

Step 14

When negotiating licence agreements, make sure that the agreement incorporates robust provisions covering privacy and confidentiality.

Step 15

Where data is housed in a data centre controlled by an external vendor, librarians should ensure that they know where it is located, and what certifications the facility has, in order to be able to ensure it meets industry best practice.

Step 16

Use http secure (https) on your websites (see https://letsencrypt.org, for example, which is a free, automated and open Certificate Authority). In addition there is the add-on HTTPS Everywhere, http://eff.org/https-everywhere, which rewrites requests to websites to ensure they use the encrypted HTTPS if they support it.

Step 17

If you are getting rid of equipment such as a photocopier, remember patron privacy. Some copiers (and other types of office equipment) have hard drives capable of storing confidential personal information, and these need to be safely wiped and destroyed. Keteyian (2010) points out that most digital copiers contain a hard drive which stores an image of every document copied, scanned or e-mailed by the machine, and that this represents a pot of gold for anyone in the identity theft business.

There are IT destruction companies that will do this for you and recycle the machinery, e.g. www.greenitrecycling.co.uk. Obviously before using any such companies you will need to make sure that you first check their data protection credentials.

This point would also cover getting rid of physical furniture. In 2017, for example, a county council was fined £60,000 for sending to a second-hand shop a cabinet which contained social work case files with sensitive information about seven children (Information Commissioner's Office, 2017b).

Step 18

Embedded content: check if your library is leaking catalogue searches to Amazon. Hellman points out that content embedded in websites is a huge source of privacy leakage in library services. 'Without meaning to, many libraries send data to Amazon about the books a user is searching for; cover images are almost always the culprit' (Hellman, 2016).

Step 19

Make sure you are using a secure form of authentication to connect with self-serve units, journal databases, e-book platforms, etc. If, for example, you are using SIP2 (Standard Interchange Protocol, a proprietary standard for communication between library computer systems and self-service circulation terminals), is it encrypted and, if so, how? Many SIP2 messages contain sensitive information that must not be exchanged without proper encryption. SIP2 does allow for encryption between host and client but it is up to the ILS vendor to provide this capability and then for individual libraries to implement it. One example of a secure method for authentication would be Open ID (https://openid.net).

Step 20

Sign up to the Library Digital Privacy Pledge, https://libraryfreedomproject. org/ourwork/digitalprivacypledge.

The Library Freedom Project developed the Library Digital Privacy Pledge for libraries, for vendors that serve libraries and for membership organisations. A key part of the pledge is to use https to deliver library services and the information resources offered by libraries.

Step 21

Librarians should use the NISO (2015) patron privacy framework to inform their actions. The framework is in the form of 12 guiding principles. They should be regarded as a starting point, because further work is required in order to make some of the principles implementable.

In any case, the 11th principle is about the need for *continuous improvement*: 'Libraries, content, and software providers should continuously assess and strive to improve user privacy as threats, technology, legal frameworks, business practices and user expectations of privacy evolve'. This recognises the way in which information management practices, security protocols and legal frameworks change over time. It follows that the way in which librarians protect patron privacy will also need to adapt and change accordingly. They will need to continually strive to improve their practices and procedures if they are to ensure that they are providing the most appropriate level of protection for their users' personal data.

Step 22

Ensure that users' print jobs can only be retrieved at the printer by swiping their library card. Sometimes library users can be their own worst enemies when it comes to protecting their privacy. Consider a situation where a library user prints out a document containing sensitive personal data. It could easily result in a data breach if they forget to collect the printout straight away. Another library user who has also sent a document to the printer might pick up the sensitive material by accident – or they could simply be quicker at getting to the printer before the original library user has had a chance to collect their own printout.

Step 23

Carry out a data protection impact assessment (DPIA) when introducing a new service or making changes to an existing service, where the processing of personal data is involved. GDPR Article 35 sets out a legal obligation to carry out a DPIA where the processing of personal data is likely to result in a high risk to the rights and freedoms of natural persons (see Chapter 10). DPIAs are used by organisations to identify, understand and address any data protection issues that might arise when they are developing new products and services or undertaking any other new activities that involve the processing of personal data. DPIAs will help to identify potentially risky data processing activities and the measures that can be taken to mitigate those risks.

It is helpful if organisations can make sure the DPIA is implemented into the general project initiation checklist of the organisation as a whole, in order to make sure it is considered at the start of a project and not as an afterthought at the end, when it is usually too late to make the changes required.

Step 24

Make use of browser add-ons which help to protect privacy, such as Privacy Badger (www.eff.org/privacybadger) or NoScript (https://noscript.net). See also the list of tools on pp. 176–9.

Step 25

If you use website analytics software, consider using software that is respectful of privacy (such as Matomo (https://matomo.org)). A useful case study is that of Cornell University Library (Chandler and Wallace, 2016), which made the switch to Piwik (which is now the priced product Matomo) from Google Analytics. Unlike remote-hosted services (such as Google Analytics, Webtrends or Adobe Analytics), Matomo is hosted locally. The data is tracked inside your Mysql database, which means that you have full control over your data.

Step 26

Check the referrer http header policy (www.w3.org/TR/referrer-policy) on your websites for outgoing requests and navigations to ensure that information is not being unintentionally leaked.

The 'Referrer' header is frequently considered to be a privacy concern. People can be surprised by the way in which the internet works. With the 'referrer' header, your browser lets a site know which website it visited last. The reason why this is such a concern regarding privacy and confidentiality is that if the site was coded carelessly, your browser may be communicating very sensitive information such as session tokens, usernames and passwords, or any other input that formed part of the URL.

CHAPTER 13

The right to be forgotten

The right to be forgotten (RTBF) means that search engines are required to remove search links when requests from citizens meet certain tests. RTBF came to prominence as a result of a European Court of Justice (ECJ) case commonly known as 'Google Spain' (Google Spain SL, Google Inc. v. Agencia Española de Protección de Datos, Mario Costeja González C131/12). This landmark ruling meant that Google, a US company, was subject to EU data protection law. In the Google Spain case, the ECJ was asked:

1 Was a search engine such as Google, headquartered outside the EU but with subsidiaries operating inside, within the scope of the data protection directive?
2 Does Google 'process' information and is it a 'data controller'?
3 Does the *derecho al olvido* (right to be forgotten) extend as far as allowing someone to apply to a search engine to have information 'consigned to oblivion', even though the information in question has been lawfully published by third parties? (Brock, 2016).

The right to be forgotten is something of a misnomer. Up to now it hasn't really been enforced in a way which leads to the material being completely removed, so that it is inaccessible anywhere around the globe. Privacy is instead achieved through 'practical obscurity', whereby the information becomes harder to find as a result of de-indexing and de-listing. In Google Spain the court said that information should not be de-indexed by a search engine if it concerned a 'public figure'.

Brock (2016) says that the basic question asked in the case was whether Google's search algorithms cause harm. If so, what should be done. The territorial scope and enforceability of legal rulings about the internet remain unresolved. There is a mismatch of the transborder flow of information and the regulatory jurisdictions. (Garton Ash, 2016, 308) believes that the RTBF raises four big closely related questions: (1) what should be removed, (2) where, (3) how, and (4) by whom.

Having been established in case law, the RTBF was then enshrined in legislation (Article 17 of the GDPR).

1. The data subject shall have the right to obtain from the controller the erasure of personal data concerning him or her without undue delay and the controller shall have the obligation to erase personal data without undue delay where one of the following grounds applies:

a) the personal data are no longer necessary in relation to the purposes for which they were collected or otherwise processed;

b) the data subject withdraws consent on which the processing is based according to point (a) of Article 6(1), or point (a) of Article 9(2), and where there is no other legal ground for the processing;

c) the data subject objects to the processing pursuant to Article 21(1) and there are no overriding legitimate grounds for the processing, or the data subject objects to the processing pursuant to Article 21(2);

d) the personal data have been unlawfully processed;

e) the personal data have to be erased for compliance with a legal obligation in Union or Member State law to which the controller is subject;

f) the personal data have been collected in relation to the offer of information society services referred to in Article 8(1).

An important question that needs to be asked is should the enforcement of justice be left to private companies? Not least because battles over privacy have become struggles over digital information rights. Brock (2016, 50) points out that a company is not a neutral arbiter as a court or civic institution is positioned to be. Courts operate on the default assumption that justice should be seen to be done unless there are compelling reasons to the contrary. A company is under no such obligation. Allowing commercial entities to enforce the law with regard to RTBF requests is highly problematic because the ultimate decision as to what to de-list and why particular requests are refused or agreed to are neither open nor transparent:

• for de-listing: a clear absence of public interest; where the personal data constitutes sensitive information; spent convictions

• against de-listing: strong public interest, the availability of alternative solutions; technical considerations.

The wording of the judgment regarding the tests to determine whether links can be removed is very vague. Appeal rates are low. Most of the time decisions don't face public scrutiny but they do shape public discourse.

Google already had notice and take-down procedures in place, such as those for bank account and credit card numbers, or images of signatures. Where an RTBF request is approved, Google doesn't routinely de-link the content globally.

This happens instead on a national or possibly a regional basis. If someone requests that bank account details be taken down, Google is hardly going to say that this should only be done at a national level rather than globally, so why is its approach different when it comes to requests for the removal of other forms of personal data?

Protection of personal data in France, Germany, Spain, and Italy, especially, has its roots in a tradition of allowing individuals to control their reputation, their image and their 'honour'.

13.1   Right of oblivion

Before the advent of the world wide web, there was a natural process whereby someone's past actions would fade from the memory. The problem is that the internet has changed all of that. Garton Ash (2016, 304) notes how the legal commentator Jeffrey Rosen observed that the indelible memory of the internet could mean that 'there are no second chances - no opportunities to escape a scarlet letter in your digital past'.

Google has changed all of our lives. But Zuboff (2019, 59) draws attention to the fact that for individuals it has meant that information that would normally age and be forgotten over a period of time now remains forever young, highlighted in the foreground of each person's digital identity. In the Google Spain case, the Spanish Data Protection Agency recognised that not all information is worthy of immortality. Some information should be forgotten because that is only human.

Shouldn't people have a right to have their past transgressions forgotten? Is it really fair for a minor misdemeanour that someone committed 20 or 30 years ago to hamper their life chances now? In January 2019 the UK Supreme Court ruled[1] in favour of three people who claimed that their lives were blighted by past minor criminal convictions, and that the way in which criminal records are disclosed to employers infringed human rights. In one example, a woman was charged with shoplifting a 99p book in 1999 while suffering from a then undiagnosed mental illness. She wanted to work as a teaching assistant, but each time she applied for positions at schools she was required to disclose her historic convictions. This meant that she had to disclose her medical history to explain those convictions.

The right of oblivion was realistic in an age of dusty newspaper print archives, but it is no longer realistic without intervention, because computers simply don't forget. Instead, the worst thing you've done is often now the first thing everyone knows about you. In fact, you may not even have done it, but when you try to put the record straight the 'Streisand effect' (see Glossary) will kick in. In 2003, the American singer-songwriter Barbra Streisand tried to suppress an online photograph documenting coastal erosion, which happened to show her seaside mansion in Malibu, California. The result of her unsuccessful suit for violation of privacy was that there was a huge amount of publicity about the very image she was trying to suppress. Before she filed her lawsuit, the photograph - one in a series of thousands showing coastal erosion - had only been downloaded from the photographer's website six times, and two of those downloads were by her lawyers. When the case became known, more than 420,000 people visited the site in one month. The fame of the 'Streisand effect' has doubtless brought many more visitors since (Garton Ash, 2016, 296).

Note

1   In the matter of an application by Lorraine Gallagher for Judicial Review (Northern Ireland) R (on the application of P, G and W) (Respondents) v. Secretary of State for the Home Department and another (Appellants) R (on the application of P) (Appellant) v. Secretary of State for the Home Department and others (Respondents) [2019] UKSC 3.

CHAPTER 14

Conclusion

Privacy really does matter. People have a right to privacy. It is enshrined in Article 8 of the European Convention on Human Rights. Libraries have an important role to play in providing an environment within which their users have the freedom to read without the fear of being judged or punished.

It is only with true privacy that individuals have the opportunity to develop. Cannataci (2016) says that 'already-recognised rights such as privacy, freedom of expression and freedom of access to information constitute a tripod of enabling rights which are best considered in the context of their usefulness in enabling a human being to develop his or her personality in the freest of manners'.

14.1   Intellectual privacy

As people grow up, they naturally want to explore every aspect of who they are, including their political beliefs, their religious beliefs and their sexuality. They use the library's resources to explore those beliefs and feelings. They will want to test the veracity and accuracy of those ideas; they will want to weigh up and consider a range of opposing viewpoints before finally reaching their own decisions. It is an ongoing process of exploration and discovery, part of trying to understand who they are and their place in the world. They might want to talk things through with a small group of close friends or family before reaching a conclusion regarding a particular political or religious issue, and this will be an important part of the development process, one in which they will cherish the privacy and intimacy of their associates before they are ready to go public about their decisions and choices. They need the freedom to be able to think through the reasons that led them to the viewpoint that they have reached and to test these out on close associates before they are ready to tell the wider world.

People may well wish to explore a wide range of perspectives in order to try and understand where they themselves stand on an issue. Consider the situation whereby a teenager wants to explore the implications of climate change. How can they possibly understand the reasons why some high-profile individuals are climate change deniers if they are not willing to read the arguments made by such people? In order to take up a particular position on an issue, especially where the issue is controversial and/or potentially divisive, people need to have the freedom to read up as widely as possible about that issue. They need to read material written by people from a range of different viewpoints. Only by doing so are they in a position to understand the arguments made by anyone who takes a different view to the one that they themselves hold. But what if people are scared of doing just that. The last thing libraries should be doing is contributing towards there being a 'chilling effect' - where the act of reading an article about a controversial issue is recorded, and that record is available to third-party organisations where none of us know how our personal data will be used.

Simply because a reader borrows a book written by a Holocaust denier, for example, does not automatically mean that the reader holds the same views. Understanding the past and present sometimes requires coming into contact with challenging or unpalatable views. It would be difficult for example to analyse or critique the reasons for the rise and opposition to Marxism or fascism if you were not able to read up about those viewpoints.

14.2   The freedom to read anonymously

There are real dilemmas arising from the desire for library users to have the freedom to read anonymously. There are circumstances in which information about someone's borrowing history or browsing history is shared with the police for law enforcement purposes. This can lead to serious consequences for the reader concerned. In the US legal case of United States v. Curtin 489 FJd 935, 956 (9th Cir. 2007), for example, the majority opinion 'held that simple possession of reading material can be evidence of a defendant's criminal intent, even without proof that the accused ever read the materials' (Benvenue, 2008).

According to Cohen (1995) 'the new information age is turning out to be as much an age of information *about* readers as an age of information *for* readers. The same technologies that have made vast amounts of information accessible in digital form are enabling information providers to amass an unprecedented wealth of data about who their customers are and what they like to read'. The point Cohen makes is that copyright management technologies in the form of digital rights management systems are being developed to enable copyright owners to monitor readers' activities in cyberspace and the uses they make of reading materials acquired there.

14.3   Potential for information about reading habits to be misused

Tech companies hoover up huge quantities of data about individuals, without the individuals affected (which is all of us) realising the true extent either of the data that has been gathered up about them, or being in a position to fully appreciate the consequences of that data being in the possession of those third parties.

The technological capabilities at the disposal of corporate entities, government and law enforcement agencies are immense. Having lots of separate pieces of information about someone can be highly dangerous. Even if every single one of the pieces of information that have been gathered is accurate and true, third parties may well join them together as though they are parts of a jigsaw puzzle and use them to create a new narrative. Some of the information may have been true some time ago, but is now no longer accurate and up to date. Third parties in possession of such data may fill in the blanks on the basis of probability. For example, saying something along the lines of '95% of people who have the characteristics A, B, C, D, E and F that you have also possess characteristics G and H'. The trouble is, what if you weren't among the 95%? What if conclusions are reached about you that are incorrect, without you even knowing that third parties have made those assumptions about you? And without giving you the opportunity to update or correct the information that they are using about you? What if this method of making assumptions is used to build up a profile about you? What if your life chances are negatively affected by those assumptions without you having an opportunity to correct them? Isolated pieces of true information about a specific individual can be joined together to tell a story, but that story may be completely untrue. Intellectual surveillance gives the watcher great power over the watched, including the power to blackmail, to persuade and to classify.

Handled responsibly, big data is a useful tool of rational decision making. Wielded unwisely, it can become an instrument of the powerful, who may turn it into a source of repression, either by simply frustrating customers and employees or, worse, by harming citizens (Mayer-Schönberger and Cukier, 2013).

Richards (2015, 95) argues that a certain kind of privacy is essential if we care about freedom of expression. This kind of privacy is different from tort privacy.[1] He calls it 'intellectual privacy', and it consists of three key elements: the freedom of thought; the right to read (and engage in intellectual exploration); and the right to communicate in confidence.

Intellectual privacy is under-appreciated and under-developed. It is essentially a zone of protection that guards our ability to make up our minds freely. More formally, intellectual privacy is the protection from surveillance or unwanted interference by others when we are engaged in the process of generating ideas and forming beliefs – when we're thinking, reading and speaking with confidants before our ideas are ready for public consumption.

Richards (2015, 96) notes how it was once difficult as a practical matter to interfere with the generation of ideas. The state, market and our social contacts could not monitor our thoughts, our reading habits and our private conversations, at least not in an efficient, comprehensive and unobstructive way. But, of course, Zuboff (2019) has pointed out the dangers of what she refers to as 'surveillance capitalism', a new economic order that claims human experience as raw material for hidden commercial practices of extraction, prediction and sales.

14.4   Where do libraries fit into the defence of privacy?

A couple of years ago, at an evening event about public libraries, I will always remember the comment of one of the attendees: 'Libraries are one of the few spaces left where you are a citizen before a consumer. That is their true appeal.'

14.4.1 The role of information professionals

Brantley (2015) observes that 'public libraries are among the last protectors of privacy in contemporary society'. Clarke (2016b) believes that it is our responsibility as information professionals to protect user privacy and confidentiality: 'If we cannot (or do not) protect the intellectual privacy of our users, then we are failing as professionals'.

If part of a library's mission is to contribute to helping people to become autonomous human beings through learning and sharing knowledge with one another without having to worry about being observed or censored, libraries should advocate for people's privacy both online and offline, as well as in all forms of communication technologies and devices (Kim, 2016, 445).

Esposito (2016) notes that librarians have misjudged things:

> Libraries have, with the best of intentions in the world, taken a strong position on privacy, and they have lost. They got the whole privacy thing all wrong. Rather than participate in the policies of their institutions and the many organizations that interact with them, they have abdicated their role and are now watching as their institutions are being colonised by commercial interests, which are no longer answerable to libraries.

Are we as information professionals doing enough to protect the privacy of our users? Tummon and McKinnon (2018) believe that protecting patron privacy and educating patrons about issues related to online privacy is important. However, many academic librarians doubt that libraries are doing all they can to protect patron privacy. Sarah Houghton (2016) says that 'There is an alarming lack of awareness about privacy issues among library staff'.

⇢ The role of the librarian in protecting user privacy

Library and information professionals have an important role to play in protecting the privacy of their users:

- They can and should provide environments, both physical and digital, where people have the freedom to seek out information without the fear of being judged or punished.
- They can raise awareness of the importance of privacy and confidentiality.
- They can offer training to users and local businesses on privacy and online safety.
- They need to work with vendors of library technology and content to ensure that privacy is baked into the products that are available on the market.
- If they identify any security vulnerabilities in vendor products, they need to work with those vendors to ensure that those vulnerabilities are properly addressed and any associated privacy risks are mitigated.

14.4.2 Legal and ethical responsibility

Protecting the privacy of library users is both an ethical and legal issue.

From an ethical standpoint, members of CILIP are required to follow CILIP's ethical framework. This says that:

> As an ethical information professional I make a commitment to uphold, promote and defend . . . (A6) the confidentiality of information provided by clients or users and the right of all individuals to privacy.
>
> (CILIP, 2018a)

'Privacy is a cornerstone of our professional ethics. . . . We have an obligation to protect the privacy of our users as a matter of principle.' (Woodward, 2007, xii). From a legal perspective, if librarians are to be law-abiding citizens then it follows that they have a responsibility to comply with privacy laws. That includes not only the data protection legislation (the DPA 2018, the GDPR and the PECR) but other laws, too, which impinge upon the privacy of individuals, such as the laws on counter-terrorism, including the government's PREVENT strategy.

14.4.3 Privacy training and awareness

Libraries can and do have a role to play in providing training on privacy issues for their users. Indeed Beckstrom (2015) goes so far as to say that 'teaching patrons how to use the internet, but not how to use it safely, is like showing someone how to drive a car, but not where the seatbelt is'.

The function libraries can perform in upholding the privacy of their users includes the role of awareness raising. For example, Anderson (2018) describes how a series of exhibits called Privacy in Public was organised in New York City libraries. The exhibition examined our relationship with data, privacy, security, and the ways in which we give – or don't give – consent for our personal data to be harvested as we go about our day-to-day business.

Another example of a library raising awareness of privacy issues is that of Princeton Public Library. In January 2019 the library hosted The Glass Room Experience, which was created by Mozilla and Tactical Tech. The Glass Room is an interactive pop-up art installation showing the impact of technology in day-to-day life. The exhibition has generated a global conversation about data and privacy. It has been hosted in libraries, schools, festivals and organisations worldwide. This is an opportunity for visitors to explore the dark side of the digital world and learn about how their data is generated, harvested, traded and sold everyday.

14.4.4 Becoming more privacy-conscious

My intention in writing this book has been to help library staff become more privacy-conscious, to have confidentiality and privacy considerations in their minds when they go about delivering the services that they offer.

Privacy is a somewhat nebulous concept. Many scholars have dedicated their entire lives to trying to understand and define precisely what privacy means. In spite of this, I have tried in this book to put together a practical guide to privacy for library and information professionals. In order to help librarians become more privacy-conscious, the book contains numerous checklists and highlights a range of useful resources – such as details of the BIC template for an RFID policy, or the ICO's sample DPIA template.

Chapter 3 provides 20 practical examples of how privacy issues can and do arise in libraries; while Chapter 12 outlines a set of 26 practical steps that libraries can take in order to help protect the privacy of their users.

14.4.5 Improving things for the future

Protecting the privacy of library users cannot simply be achieved as some kind of tick-box exercise, where you work your way through a checklist of best practices. It is instead about having a mindset attuned to user privacy and confidentiality. It requires libraries to carry out privacy audits, and to undertake data protection impact assessments when new services are about to be introduced. These audits and impact assessments will draw attention to any weaknesses and vulnerabilities in the library's systems and procedures. In order to improve things for the future, strengthening the protection of user privacy, it requires having an open mind, and a genuine willingness to learn any lessons that were flagged up by the audits and DPIAs - for example, by ensuring that any steps recommended by the DPIA are implemented. Improving things for the future is all about learning from any mistakes, however big or small.

One way of protecting user privacy is to regularly undertake penetration testing and network security checks (using ethical hackers). Another way of improving the way in which a library protects the privacy of its users is to consider the sorts of areas that the library users as data subjects typically complain about:

- subject access
- disclosure of data
- security
- inaccurate data
- fair processing information not provided
- right to prevent processing
- use of data
- obtaining data
- excessive/irrelevant data
- retention of data.

If you have had complaints about any privacy- or information security-related matters, how did you handle them? Are there any lessons that can be learnt from those complaints, which can help improve your library's practices and procedures for protecting the privacy of those who use your service?

Protecting the privacy of library users is a continuous process. Information management practices, security protocols and legal frameworks change over time. Even if you think you have found the optimal way in which users' privacy can be protected, the reality is that this will only relate to a specific point in time. The nature and severity of the potential threats to user privacy will undoubtedly change over time. What works for one library may not be the complete solution for another library. Every library is different. The nature of the library buildings and their layout will differ. The mix of external vendors and third parties will differ.

⊷Privacy Principle on Public Access in Libraries

Individuals have the right to privacy when they seek information using the Internet. Internet users in public venues such as libraries must not be subject to surveillance of their activities.

(Dynamic Coalition on Public Access in Libraries (DC PAL), 2016)

14.4.6 Give library users control over how their personal data is used

Library and information professionals are committed to protecting the privacy of their users. However, it is important to acknowledge that there are services which can be offered to users in exchange for them giving up a little bit of their privacy. The key issues here are:

- Does the library user want to benefit from those services?
- Are you making them aware of the privacy implications of doing so?
- Are they in a position to make an informed and meaningful choice?

Ultimately it is for the user to decide whether it is worth losing some privacy in exchange for a more personalised and tailored library service. A couple of years ago Kate Davis (2016) said 'I want my library to exploit my borrowing data the way Amazon exploits my purchasing data. Sell to me library! Sell to me!' So, there are undoubtedly people who are keen for their personal data to be used so that they can, for example, find out about similar books to the ones that they have already read; new titles that have just been published and which are now available in the library on topics that they are particularly interested in. To achieve this requires the user to give up a little bit of their privacy in exchange for being offered a more tailored service that is highly relevant to them and their interests. That is absolutely fine, so long as:

- the user has been given the option of whether or not to sign up to the more tailored service
- you have given them adequate information about any privacy implications, so that they are genuinely making an informed choice
- everything is done transparently.

Note

1 'Tort privacy protects against emotional injury and was directed by design against disclosures of true, embarrassing facts by the media' (Richards, 2011).

CHAPTER 15

Further reading, toolkits and other resources

15.1 Books and reports on privacy in libraries
Charillon, A. (2018) *Leading the Way: a guide to privacy for public library staff,* CILIP, Newcastle Libraries and Carnegie UK.
Fernandez, P. D. and Tilton, K. (2018) *Applying Library Values to Emerging Technology: decision-making in the age of open access, maker spaces, and the ever-changing library,* ACRL Publications in Librarianship no. 72.
Givens, C. L. (2015) *Information Privacy Fundamentals for Librarians and Information Professionals,* Rowman & Littlefield.
Korn, N. and Tullo, C. (2018) *A Practical Guide to Data Protection for Information Professionals,* CILIP and Naomi Korn Copyright and Compliance.
Newman, B. and Tijerina, B. (2017) *Protecting Patron Privacy: a LITA guide,* Rowman & Littlefield.
Pedley, P. (2017) Relevance of Privacy for Corporate Library and Information Services, *Business Information Review,* **34** (1), 9-14.
Woodward, J. A. (2007) *What Every Librarian Should Know About Electronic Privacy,* Libraries Unlimited.
Zimmer, M. and Tijerina, B. (2018) *Library Values and Privacy in Our National Digital Strategies: field guides, convenings, and conversations,* National Leadership Grant For Libraries Award Report.

15.2 Checklists
Krantz, P. (2016) *Protection of Privacy in the Library Environment,* Twitter feed.

15.3 Web links
Website	URL
AboutCookies.org	www.aboutcookies.org
American Civil Liberties Union	www.aclu.org
Bits of Freedom	www.bof.nl
Book Industry Communication	www.bic.org.uk

Brussels Privacy Hub	www.brusselsprivacyhub.org
CAGE	www.cage.ngo
Campaign for Reader Privacy	www.readerprivacy.org
Choose Privacy Week	http://chooseprivacyweek.org
Common Thread Network	www.commonthreadnetwork.org
Cryptoparty	www.cryptoparty.in
Cyberwatching EU	www.cyberwatching.eu
Data Privacy Project	www.dataprivacyproject.org
Data security incident trends, ICO	https://ico.org.uk/action-weve-taken/data-security-incident-trends
Datonomy	http://datonomy.eu
Decode	www.decodeproject.eu
Digital Security Helpline	www.accessnow.org/help
Digital Unite	www.digitalunite.com
Digitale Gesellschaft	https://digitalgesellschaft.de
Don't Spy On Us	www.dontspyonus.org.uk
EBLIDA	www.eblida.org
EDRI	https://edri.org
Electronic Frontier Foundation	www.eff.org www.eff.org/issues/privacy
Electronic Privacy Information Center	www.epic.org
European Interactive Digital Advertising Alliance	www.edaa.eu
Frontline Defenders	www.frontlinedefenders.org
GetLinkInfo	www.getlinkinfo.com
Global Compliance Resource Center	https://ciphercloud.com/resources/global-compliance-resource-center
Go to Hellman	http://go-to-hellman-blogspot.com
Harvard University Privacy Tools Project	https://privacytools.seas.harvard.edu
Haveibeenpwned	www.haveibeenpwned.com
How privacy friendly is your site?	http://webbkoll.dataskydd.net/en
HTTPS grading of UK public libraries	www.librarieshacked.org/tutorials/httpsgrading
Identity Theft Resource Center	www.idtheftcenter.org

IFLA FAIFE	www.ifla.org/faife
Information Privacy Law	www.informationprivacylaw.com
International Association of Privacy Professionals	www.iapp.org
International Association of Privacy Professionals resources	www.iapp.org/resources
La Quadrature du Net and Access	www.laquadrature.net/en
Let's Encrypt	www.letsencrypt.org
Libraries Guide To Patron Privacy	http://patronprivacy.herokuapp.com/
Library app security	www.librarieshacked.org/articles/libraryappsecurity
Library Freedom Project	https://libraryfreedomproject.org
Mailbox.org	https://mailbox.org
Manila Principles On Intermediary Liability	http://manilaprinciples.org
Mobile app security	www.librarieshacked.org/articles/mobileappsecurity
NakedCitizens.eu	http://nakedcitizens.eu
Nymity GDPR toolkit	www.nymity.com/gdpr-toolkit/download.aspx
OnGuard Online	www.consumer.ftc.gov/features/feature-0038-onguardonline
Open Rights Group	www.openrightsgroup.org
Panopticon Blog	http://panopticonblog.com
Panoptykon Foundation	https://en.panoptykon.org
Pep Foundation	www.pep-project.org/2016-02
PersonalData.IO	www.personaldata.io
Privacy in Libraries in the Digital Age	http://libraryprivacy.tumblr.com
Privacy International	www.privacyinternational.org
Privacy News Headlines	https://privacynewshighlights.wordpress.com
Privacy Rights Clearinghouse	http://privacyrights.org/data-breach
Privacy SOS	http://privacysos.org
Privacy tools	www.privacytools.io
Privacy Training Center	www.privacytraining.org
Privacy, Compliance & Data Security Association	http://finallypcds.org

Ranking Digital Rights	www.rankingdigitalrights.org
Reset the Net	www.resetthenet.org
Right to Information – good law and practice	www.right2info.org
Stay Safe Online	https://staysafeonline.org
Surveillance Self Defense	https://ssd.eff.org/en
Tactical Technology Collective	https://tacticaltech.org
Teaching Privacy Project	www.teachingprivacy.org
Terms of Service Didn't Read project	https://tosdr.org
Tor Project	www.torproject.org
TrustArc consumer resources	www.trustarc.com/consumer-resources
Usable Privacy Policy research project	http://usableprivacy.org
Your Choices Online	www.youronlinechoices.eu and www.youronlinechoices.com/uk/ helpful-videos

15.4   Toolkits

Scottish PEN (2018) *Libraries for Privacy - a Digital Security and Privacy Toolkit:* protecting library staff and users in the age of big data, Scottish PEN in collaboration with Library Freedom Project, CILIP Scotland, Scottish Library & Information Council.

15.5   Tools

Ad blockers	
Adblock Plus	https://adblockplus.org
Adblocker	https://chrome.google.com/webstore/detail/ adblocker-for-chrome- kfeabeiebipdmaenpmbgknjce?hl=en
Ghostery	www.ghostery.com
Analyse data traffic	
Datapp	http://datapp.fr/site
Lightbeam	https://addons.mozilla.org/en-GB/ firefox/addon/lightbeam
Tcpdump	www.tcpdump.org
Wireshark	www.wireshark.org

Analytics	
Google Analytics opt-out	https://tools.google.com/dlpage/gaoptout
Matomo	https://matomo.org
Antivirus	
ClamAV	www.clamav.net
Malwarebytes	www.malwarebytes.com
Block third-party cookies	
Crumble	Available from the Chrome Store, https://chrome.google.com/webstore/
uBlock Origin	https://github.com/gorhill/uBlock
Browsers	
Tor	www.torproject.org/projects/torbrowser.html.en
Orfox	https://guardianproject.info/apps/orfox/
Safari	www.apple.com/safari
Browser add-ons	
Forget That Page Chrome Extension	https://seo-michael.co.uk/forget-that-page-for-chrome
Panopticlick	https://panopticlick.eff.org
Privacy Badger	www.eff.org/privacybadger
Trackmenot	https://cs.nyu.edu/trackmenot
Cleaners	
Bleachbit	www.bleachbit.org
Ccleaner	www.ccleaner.com
Cleanslate	www.fortresgrand.com/products/cls/cls.htm
Deepfreeze	www.faronics.com/en-uk/home
Disk/drive encryption	
Bitlocker (Windows)	https://docs.microsoft.com/en-us/windows/security/information-protection/bitlocker/bitlocker-overview
Filevault (OS X)	https://support.apple.com/en-gb/HT204837
LUKS (GNU/Linux)	https://gitlab.com/cryptsetup/cryptsetup
E-mail	
Discard.email	https://addons.mozilla.org/en-US/firefox/addon/discardemail
Enigmail	www.enigmail.net/index.php/en
Hushmail	www.hushmail.com
OpenPGP	www.openpgp.org

Proton Mail	https://protonmail.com
Tutanota	https://tutanota.com
Encryption	
Adium	https://adium.im
Certbot	Enables https on website. https://certbot.eff.org
HTTPS Everywhere	http://eff.org/https-everywhere
Let's Encrypt	https://letsencrypt.org
Pidgin	http://pidgin-encrypt.sourceforge.net
Veracrypt	www.veracrypt.fr/en/Downloads.html
Operating systems	
Qubes	www.qubes-os.org
Replicant	https://replicant.us/freedom-privacy-security-issues.php
Subgraph	https://subgraph.com/sgos
TAILS	Operating system (live). https://tails.boum.org
Password managers	
1Password	https://1password.com
Blur	https://abine.com/index.html
KeepassX	www.keepassx.org
LastPass	www.lastpass.com
Personal data store	
Mydex	https://mydex.org
openPDS	http://openpds.media.mit.edu
Remove information	
DeleteMe	Remove personal information from search engines. https://abine.com/index.html
Fileshredder.org	Shred unwanted files. www.fileshredder.org/
Script safety	
Noscript	https://noscript.net
Scriptsafe	https://addons.mozilla.org/en-US/firefox/addon/script-safe
Search engines	
Disconnect Search	https://search.disconnect.me
Duckduckgo	https://duckduckgo.com
Oscobo	www.oscobo.com
Peekier	www.peekier.com
Qwant	www.qwant.com/?l=en

Search Incognito	www.searchincognito.com
Startpage	https://startpage.com
Tools to rate/check privacy robustness	
Privacy Grade	http://privacygrade.org
SSL Labs	Test the TLS/SSL security of a website or browser. www.ssllabs.com
TOSDR (Terms of service didn't read)	Rates and labels website terms and privacy policies from very good to very bad. www.tosdr.org
Webbkoll	Check how good on data protection your website is. https://webbkoll.dataskydd.net/sv
VPN	
Bitmask	https://bitmask.net
Hotspot Shield	www.hotspotshield.com
Open VPN	https://openvpn.net
Private Internet Access	www.privateinternetaccess.com
Riseup's VPN	https://riseup.net/en/vpn
Tunnelbear	www.tunnelbear.com
Other	
Anonymouse	Ad-free anonymous searching. http://anonymouse.org
FaceNiff	Android app allowing you to sniff and intercept web session profiles. http://faceniff.ponury.net
IP location	www.iplocation.net
Ninja Proxy	https://ninjaproxyserver.com
Sandstorm	Self-host web apps. https://sandstorm.io
Signal private messenger	https://signal.org
SMAC	MAC address spoofing. https://smac.en.downloadastro.com
Tracking Observer	Web tracking detection platform. https://trackingobserver.cs.washington.edu/
Web of Trust	Safe web searching and browsing www.mywot.com.

Works cited and further reading

Adams, H. R. (2008) How Circulation Systems May Impact Student Privacy, *School Library Media Activities Monthly*, **24** (6), 36.

American Library Association (2006) *Questions and Answers on Privacy and Confidentiality*, www.ala.org/Template.cfm?Section=interpretations&Template=/ContentManagement/ContentDisplay.cfm&ContentID=15347.

American Library Association (2015) *Library Privacy Guidelines for E-book Lending and Digital Content Vendors*, www.ala.org/advocacy/libraryprivacyguidelinesebooklendinganddigitalcontentvendors.

American Library Association (2016a) *Library Privacy Guidelines for Data Exchange Between Networked Devices and Services*, www.ala.org/advocacy/privacy/guidelines/dataexchange.

American Library Association (2016b) *Library Privacy Guidelines for Library Management Systems*, www.ala.org/advocacy/libraryprivacyguidelineslibrarymanagementsystems.

American Library Association (2016c) *Library Privacy Guidelines for Library Websites, OPACs, and Discovery Services*, www.ala.org/advocacy/privacy/guidelines/OPAC.

American Library Association (2016d) *Library Privacy Guidelines For Public Access Computers and Networks*, www.ala.org/advocacy/privacy/guidelines/public-access-computer.

American Library Association (2016e) *Library Privacy Guidelines for Students in K-12 Schools*, https://chooseprivacyeveryday.org/resources/guidelines-checklists-for-libraries/library-privacy-guidelines-for-students-in-k-12-schools.

American Library Association (2017) *Suggested Guidelines: how to respond to law enforcement requests for library records and user information*, www.ala.org/advocacy/privacy/lawenforcement/guidelines.

Anderson, D. E. (2018) Privacy in Public: a new exhibit at a library near you, *Medium*, 17 December, https://medium.com/the-bytegeist-blog/privacy-in-public-a-new-exhibit-at-a-library-near-you-1797592923b3.

Angwin, J. (2014) *Dragnet Nation: a quest for privacy, security and freedom in a world of relentless surveillance*, Henry Holt.

Archer, J. (2018) Heathrow Airport Fined £120,000 for 'Serious' Data Breach, *The Telegraph*, 8 October.

Ard, B. J. (2013) Confidentiality and the Problem of Third Parties: protecting reader privacy in the age of intermediaries, *Yale Journal of Law and Technology*, **16** (1), 1-58.

Article 29 Data Protection Working Party (2017) *Guidelines on Data Protection Impact Assessment (DPIA) and Determining Whether Processing is 'Likely to Result in a High Risk' for the Purposes of Regulation 2016/679*, European Commission, https://ec.europa.eu/newsroom/article29/item-detail.cfm?item_id=611236.

Balas, J. L. (2005) Should There be an Expectation of Privacy in the Library?, *Computers in Libraries*, **25** (6), 33-5.

Ballard, M. (2006) Schools Can Fingerprint Children Without Parental Consent: DfES qualifies its stance, *The Register*, 7 September, www.theregister.co.uk/2006/09/07/kiddyprinting_allowed.

Barron, S. and Preater, A. (2018) Critical Systems Librarianship. In Nicholson, K. and Seale, M. (eds), *The Politics of Theory and the Practice of Critical Librarianship*, Library Juice Press.

BBC News Online (2011) Snooping Devices Found in Cheshire Library Computers, 8 February, www.bbc.co.uk/news/uk-england-manchester-12396799.

Beckstrom, M. (2015) *Protecting Patron Privacy: safe practices for public computers*, Libraries Unlimited.

Belveze, D. (2017) *Programming Cryptoparties in Libraries: how librarians can contribute to students and citizens empowerment against tracking and mass-surveillance*, https://hal.archives-ouvertes.fr/hal-01504076

Benvenue, A. L. (2008) Possession of Reading Material and Intent to Commit a Crime in United States v. Curtin, *Ninth Circuit Survey*, **38** (3), http://digitalcommons.law.ggu.edu/ggulrev/vol38/iss3/7.

Bernbach, R. (2016) The Library of Congress was Hacked Because It Hasn't Joined the Digital Age, *Motherboard*, 15 September.

BiblioCommons (2016) *Essential Digital Infrastructure for Public Libraries in England: a plan moving forward*, http://goscl.com/wpcontent/uploads/151130DigitalPlatformFinalReport.pdf.

Bibliotheca (2016) Cloud library, www.bibliotheca.com/3/index.php/enuk/oursolutions/cloudlibrary.

BigBrotherWatch (2015) *A Breach of Trust: how local authorities commit 4 data breaches every day*, www.bigbrotherwatch.org.uk/wp-content/uploads/2015/08/A-Breach-of-Trust.pdf.

BigBrotherWatch (2018) *Cyber Attacks in Local Authorities: how the quest for big data is threatening cyber security*, https://bigbrotherwatch.org.uk/wp-content/uploads/2018/02/Cyber-attacks-in-local-authorities.pdf.

BIIA (2016) *Human Error Fuels Most Data Breaches*, Business Information Industry Association.

Billingsley, E. (2016) Malibu Library Course Provides Cybersecurity Basics for Teens, *Malibu Surfside News*, 29 December.

Bloomberg Law and International Association of Privacy Professionals (2016) *Assessing and Mitigating Privacy Risk Starts at the Top.*

Booth, J. (2004) UK 'Sleepwalking into a Stasi State', *The Guardian*, 16 August.

Brantley, P. (2015) Books and Browsers, *Publishers Weekly*, 2 January.

Breeding, M. (2016) Data from Library Implementations, *Library Technology Report*, **52** (4), 29-35.

Briney, K. (2018) Student Learning Analytics in Libraries - Thoughts and Resources, *Love Data Week*, 13 February.

British Library (2016) *Annual Report 2015/2016.*

Brock, G. (2016) *The Right to be Forgotten: privacy and the media in the digital age*, I. B. Tauris.

Brown, F. (2014) Outsourcing Law Firm Libraries to Commercial Law Library and Legal Research Services: the UK experience, *Australian Academic & Research Libraries*, **45** (3), 176-92, doi:http://dx.doi.org/10.1080/00048623.2014.920130

Brunton, F. and Nissenbaum, H. (2013) Political and Ethical Perspectives on Data Obfuscation. In Hildebrandt, M. and de Vries, K. (eds), *Privacy, Due Process and the Computational Turn: the philosophy of law meets the philosophy of technology*, Routledge, 171-95.

Bundesministerium der Justiz und für Verbraucherschutz (2017) *Bundesdatenschutzgesetz (BDSG)*, (English version), www.gesetze-im-internet.de/englisch_bdsg.

Buschman, J. (2016) The Structural Irrelevance of Privacy: a provocation, *Library Quarterly*, **86** (4), 419-33.

Bussee, K. and Hellekson, K. (2012) Identity, Ethics, and Fan Privacy. In Larsen, K. and Zubernis, L. (eds), *Fan Culture: theory/practice*, Cambridge Scholars Publishing.

Caldwell-Stone, D. (2012) A Digital Dilemma: ebooks and users' rights, *American Libraries*, 29 May, https://americanlibrariesmagazine.org/2012/05/29/a-digital-dilemma-ebooks-and-users-rights.

Caldwell-Stone, D. (2019) *New Library Bill of Rights Provision Recognizes and Defends Library Users Privacy*, ALA press release, February, www.ala.org/news/press-releases/2019/02/new-library-bill-rights-provision-recognizes-and-defends-library-users.

Campbell, D. G. and Cowan, S. R. (2016) The Paradox of Privacy: revisiting a core library value in an age of big data and linked data, *Library Trends*, **64** (3), 492-511.

Cannataci, J. A. (2016) *Report of the Special Rapporteur on the Right to Privacy,*

(Human Rights Council Thirty-First session. Agenda item 3 A/HRC/31/64), United Nations.

Caro, A. and Markman, C. (2016) Measuring Library Vendor Cyber Security: seven easy questions every librarian can ask, *Code4lib*, **32**, http://journal.code4lib.org/articles/11413.

Carpenter, T. (2016) Twitter (@TAC_NISO), 18 August.

Carr, N. (2009) *Cloud Computing*, https://britannica.com/technology/cloud-computing.

Chalfant, M. (2017) Dow Jones Customer Data Exposed in Cloud Error, *The Hill*, 17 July.

Chandler, A. and Wallace, M. (2016) Using Piwik Instead of Google Analytics at the Cornell University Library, *Serials Librarian*, **71** (3-4), 173-9, doi:10.1080/0361526X.2016.1245645.

Charillon, A. (2018) *Leading the Way: a guide to privacy for public library staff*, CILIP, Newcastle Libraries and Carnegie UK Trust.

Chozick, A. and Protess, B. (2013) Privacy Breach on Bloomberg's Data Terminals, *New York Times*, 10 May, www.nytimes.com/2013/05/11/business/media/privacy-breach-on-bloombergs-data-terminals.html.

CILIP (2011) *User Privacy in Libraries: guidelines for the reflective practitioner*, rev. edn, https://archive.cilip.org.uk/sites/default/files/documents/Privacy_June_AW.pdf.

CILIP (2018a) *Ethical Framework*.

CILIP (2018b) *Ethical Framework: clarifying notes*.

CILIP (2019) Spending Cuts Continue to Bite as Public Libraries Suffer Again – CIPFA, *Information Professional*, January/February, 5.

Clarke, I. (2016a) Public Libraries, Police and the Normalisation of Surveillance, *Infoism*, 24 August, http://infoism.co.uk/2016/09/police-libraries.

Clarke, I. (2016b) The Digital Divide in the Post Snowden Era, *Journal of Radical Librarianship*, **2**, 1-32.

Clarke, R. (1997) Introduction to Dataveillance and Information Privacy, and Definitions of Terms, *Roger Clarke's blog*, www.rogerclarke.com/DV/Intro.html.

Cobain, I. (2016) Jo Cox Killed in 'Brutal, Cowardly' and Politically Motivated Murder, Trial Hears, *The Guardian*, 14 November.

Cohen, J. E. (1995) A Right to Read Anonymously: a closer look at 'copyright management' in cyberspace, *Connecticut Law Review*, **28**, 981.

Coleman, T. and Levine, J. (2015) ALA's Facebook Account was Hacked and you'll Never Guess What Happened Next!, *American Libraries Magazine*, 15 September.

Collier, B. (2017) Cameras in Library Bathroom Cause Privacy Concerns: the use of cameras has people questioning why they are needed, *Ourquadcities.com*, 13 January.

Conger, S., Pratt, J. H. and Loch, K. D. (2013) Personal Information Privacy and Emerging Technologies, *Information Systems Journal*, **23**, 401-17.

Cooke, L., Spacey, R., Creaser, C. and Muir, A. (2014) 'You Don't Come to the Library to Look at Porn and Stuff Like That': filtering software in public libraries, *Library and Information Research*, **38** (117).

Cowell, J. (2016) Twitter (@janecowell8), 16 August, https://twitter.com/janecowell8/status/765579046306668544.

Cox, J. (2019) Education and Science Giant Elsevier Left Users' Passwords Exposed Online, *Motherboard*, 18 March, www.vice.com/en_us/article/vbw8b9/elsevier-user-passwords-exposed-online.

Curry, A. (2005) If I Ask, Will They Answer? Evaluating public library reference service to gay and lesbian youth, *Reference & User Services Quarterly*, **45** (1) (Fall 2005), 65-75, www.jstor.org/stable/20864443.

Cyrus, J. W. and Baggett, M. P. (2012) Mobile Technology: implications for privacy and librarianship, *Reference Librarian*, **53** (3), 284-96, doi:10.1080/02763877.2012.678765.

Data Protection Commissioner (Ireland) (2017) *Annual Report*.

Davis, K. (2016) Twitter (@katiedavis), 29 August.

De Mar, C. (2018) Should Book Choices be Private? Harold Washington library patron calls for change, *CBS Chicago*, 29 November.

Dissent (2007) CASSIE and Library Privacy Questions, *Chronicles of Dissent*, 23 May.

Dixon, P. (2006) Ethical Issues Implicit in Library Authentication and Access Management: risks and best practices, *Journal of Library Administration*, **47** (3-4), 142-62, doi:10.1080/01930820802186480.

Dressler, V. and Kristof, C. (2018) The Right to be Forgotten and Implications on Digital Archives: a survey of ARL member institutions on practice and policy, *College & Research Libraries*, **79** (7), https://doi.org/10.5860/crl.79.7.972.

Dynamic Coalition on Public Access in Libraries (DC PAL) (2016) *Principles on Public Access in Libraries*, IFLA. www.ifla.org/files/assets/hq/topics/info-society/documents/handout-principles-on-public-access-in-libraries.pdf.

Economist (2017) The World's Most Valuable Resource is No Longer Oil, but Data, *The Economist*, 6 May.

Edwards, L. (2016) Twitter (@lilian_edwards), 13 July.

Esposito, J. (2016) Libraries May Have Gotten the Privacy Thing All Wrong, *The Scholarly Kitchen*, 23 June, https://scholarlykitchen.sspnet.org/2016/06/23/libraries-may-have-gotten-the-privacy-thing-all-wrong.

European Commission. Enterprise and Industry Directorate-General (2008) *Standardisation Mandate to the European Standardisation Organisations CEN, CENELEC and ETSI in the Field of Information and Communication Technologies Applied to Radio Frequency Identification (RFID) and Systems*.

Express (2016) Police Force to Trial Using Library Staff to help the Public Report Crimes, *The Express*, 23 August, www.express.co.uk/news/uk/703088/police-trial-library-staff-public-report-crimes.

Fillo, M. E. (1999) Privacy Concern, Printer Control Clash at Library, *Hartford Courant*, 17 February.

Finn, R., Wright, D. and Friedewald, M. (2013) Seven Types of Privacy. In Gutwirth, S. (ed.), *European Data Protection: coming of age*, Dordrecht, Springer Science & Business Media, doi:10.1007/978-94-007-5170-5_1.

Floridi, L. (2014) *The Fourth Revolution: on the impact of information and communication technologies*, Oxford University Press.

Foerstel, H. N. (1991) *Surveillance in the Stacks: the FBI's library awareness program*, Greenwood Press.

Freeman, M. (2016) Yarm Library Co-locates with Newcastle Building Society, *Libraries TaskForce blog*, 12 December, https://librariestaskforce.blog.gov.uk/2016/12/12/yarm-library-co-locates-with-newcastle-building-society.

Gallagher, S. (2017) Man Finds USB Stick with Heathrow Security Plans, Queen's Travel Details, *Ars Technica*, 30 October, https://arstechnica.com/information-technology/2017/10/man-finds-usb-stick-with-heathrow-security-plans-queens-travel-details.

Gangadharan, S. P. (2017) Library Privacy in Practice: system change and challenges, *I/S: A Journal of Law and Policy for the Information Society*, **13** (1), 175-98.

Garcia-Febo, L., Hustad, A., Rosch, H., Sturges, P. and Vallotton, A. (2012) *IFLA Code of Ethics for Librarians and Other Information Workers*, IFLA FAIFE, www.ifla.org/publications/node/11092.

Garton Ash, T. (2016) *Free Speech: ten principles for a connected world*, Yale University Press.

Gaudin, S. (2016) New York Public Library Reads Up on the Cloud, *ComputerWorld*, 25 August.

Givens, C. (2015) Working on a Privacy Policy for Your Library? Read these inspiring examples first, *The Booklist Reader*, 8 January.

Gorman, M. (2000) *Our Enduring Values: librarianship in the 21st century*, ALA Editions.

Gorman, M. (2015) *Our Enduring Values Revisited: librarianship in an ever-changing world*, ALA Editions.

Gough, K. (2014) San Diego State University, *Privacy Rights Clearinghouse*, 27 May.

Green, B., Cunningham, G., Ekblaw, A., Kominers, P., Linzer, A. and Crawford, S. (2017) *Open Data Privacy*, Berkman Klein Center for Internet & Society Research Publication,
https://cyber.harvard.edu/publications/2017/02/opendataprivacypla.

Green, D. A. (2016) Leaks and Liberty: policy and legal consequences of unauthorised big data releases, *Financial Times*, David Allen Green's blog, 12 April, www.ft.com/content/69d2ac1b-ebaa-339d-9750-4105cf4ebf3f.

Greiner, T. (2013) Hold That Book, But You're Risking Your Privacy, *The Oregonian*, 12 July.

Griffin, A. (2015) Stingray Fake Phone Masts Placed Around London to Listen in on All Calls, *The Independent*, 10 June, www.independent.co.uk/life-style/gadgets-and-tech/news/stingray-fake-phone-masts-placed-around-london-to-listen-in-on-all-calls-10309706.html.

Ha, T.-H. (2016) These are the Books Hillary Clinton Has Been Borrowing from the Library, *Quartz*, 12 October.

Hawley, Z. (2017) Councils Slammed Over Libraries Shake-up, *Derby Evening Telegraph*, 25 September.

Hawley, Z. (2018) £400k Gets Handover of City Libraries Back on Track, *Derby Evening Telegraph*, 6 December.

Hedtke, L. P. (2007) Cereal Boxes and Milk Crates: zine libraries and infoshops are . . . now, *LIBREAS, Library ideas*, **12**, 40–3.

Hellman, E. (2016) How to Check if Your Library is Leaking Catalogue Searches to Amazon, *Go-to-hellman*, 22 December,
https://go-to-hellman.blogspot.com/2016/12/how-to-check-if-your-library-is-leaking.html.

Henderson, R. (1991) Russian Political Emigrés and the British Museum Library, *Library History*, **9** (1–2), 59–68, doi:10.1179/lib.1991.9.1–2.59.

Home Office (2018) *Covert Human Intelligence Sources: revised code of practice*,
https://assets.publishing.service.gov.uk/government/uploads/system/uploads/attachment_data/file/742042/20180802_CHIS_code_.pdf.

Houghton, S. (2016) Twitter (@TheLib), 28 October,
https://twitter.com/TheLiB/status/792060405296148480.

Information Commissioner's Office (2014a) *Conducting Privacy Impact Assessments: code of practice*.

Information Commissioner's Office (2014b) *Protecting Personal Data in Online Services: learning from the mistakes of others*, https://ico.org.uk/media/1042221/protecting-personal-data-in-online-services-learning-from-the-mistakes-of-others.pdf.

Information Commissioner's Office (2016) *Bring Your Own Device (BYOD)*, https://ico.org.uk/media/for-organisations/documents/1563/ico_bring_your_own_device_byod_guidance.pdf.

Information Commissioner's Office (2017a) *In the Picture: a data protection code of practice for surveillance cameras and personal information*, https://ico.org.uk/media/for-organisations/documents/1542/cctv-code-of-practice.pdf.

Information Commissioner's Office (2017b) Council Fined for Leaving Sensitive Files in Cabinet Sent to Second Hand Shop, https://ico.org.uk/about-the-ico/news-and-events/news-and-blogs/2017/03/council-fined-for-leaving-sensitive-files-in-cabinet-sent-to-second-hand-shop.

Information Commissioner's Office (2018a) *Data Protection Impact Assessments*, https://ico.org.uk/for-organisations/guide-to-data-protection/guide-to-the-general-data-protection-regulation-gdpr/accountability-and-governance/data-protection-impact-assessments.

Information Commissioner's Office (2018b) *Sample DPIA Template*, https://ico.org.uk/media/about-the-ico/consultations/2258461/dpia-template-v04-post-comms-review-20180308.pdf.

Iron Mountain and Association for Information and Image Management (2015) *What Will it Take to be a NextGen InfoPro?*, AIIM white paper, https://info.aiim.org/what-will-it-take-to-be-a-nextgen-infopro.

IT World (2012) What Makes a Cloud a Cloud? 5 defining characteristics, *IT World*, 12 April, www.itworld.com/article/2729056/cloud-computing/what-makes-a-cloud-a-cloud–5–defining-characterstics.html.

Johnston, S. D. (2000) Rethinking Privacy in the Public Library, *International Information & Library Review*, **32** (3–4), 509–17.

Jones, K. M. and Salo, D. (2018) Learning Analytics and the Academic Library: professional ethics commitments at a crossroads, *College & Research Libraries*, **79** (3), 304–23.

Keizer, G. (2012) *Privacy*, Picador.

Keteyian, A. (2010) Digital Photocopiers Loaded With Secrets, *CBS News*, 19 April.

Khan, A. (2016) The Future of Libraries in the Digital Age, *CILIP Update*, December/January, 44–5.

Kim, B. (2016) Cybersecurity and Digital Surveillance Versus Usability and Privacy, *C&RL News*, October (ACRL TechConnect).

Kingsley-Hughes, A. (2011) Has Amazon and Overdrive 'Screwed' the Libraries? Maybe, maybe not: or do libraries have to move with the time?

ZDNet, 21 October, www.zdnet.com/article/has-amazon-and-overdrive-screwed-the-libraries-maybe-maybe-not.

Kirk, T. (2016) Jo Cox Trial: 'Right-wing nationalist Thomas Mair looked up Ku Klux Klan and Nazis before killing MP', *London Evening Standard*, 14 November.

Koops, B.-J. (2011) Forgetting Footprints, Shunning Shadows: a critical analysis of the 'right to be forgotten' in Big Data practice, *SCRIPTed*, **8** (3), 229–56, doi.org/10.2139/ssrn.1986719.

Koops, B.-J., Newell, B. C., Timan, T., Skorvanek, I., Chokrevski, T. and Galic, M. (2017) A Typology of Privacy, *University of Pennsylvania Journal of International Law*, **38** (2), 483–575, https://scholarship.law.upenn.edu/cgi/viewcontent.cgi?article=1938.

Lally, C. (2017) Ex-partner of London Attacker is 'Deeply Shocked' by his Actions, *Irish Times*, 7 June, www.irishtimes.com/news/crime-and-law/ex-partner-of-london-attacker-is-deeply-shocked-by-his-actions-1.3110671.

Lambert, A. D., Parker, M. and Bashir, M. (2015) Library Patron Privacy in Jeopardy: an analysis of the privacy polices of digital content vendors, *ASIST*, 6–10 November.

Lambert, T. (2016) Facing Privacy Issues: your face as big data, *Public Libraries Online*, 19 May.

Lanier, J. (2018) *Ten Arguments for Deleting Your Social Media Accounts Right Now*, Bodley Head.

Lenters, M. (2019) The Age of Surveillance Capitalism: how companies undermine your sovereignty for profit, *Innovation Origins*, 31 January, https://innovationorigins.com/the-age-of-surveillance-capitalism-how-companies-undermine-your-sovereignty-for-profit.

Lepore, T. (2017) Brighton Library Installs Sound Masking System to Provide Privacy in Open-plan Rooms, *PSN Europe*, 15 August.

Lincolnshire County Council (2016) *Malicious Software (Malware) Attack on Lincolnshire County Council, 26th January 2016*, Report, https://www.lincolnshire.gov.uk/Download/97801.

Lincolnshire Echo (2012) Issue of CRB Checks in Local Libraries, *Lincolnshire Echo*, 23 August, 52.

McCurry, J. (2015) Librarians in Uproar After Borrowing Record of Haruki Murakami is Leaked, *The Guardian*, 2 December.

McDonald, A. and Cranor, L. F. (2008) The Cost of Reading Privacy Policies, *I/S: a journal of law and policy for the information society*, **4** (3).

McGovern, M. (2016) The University, PREVENT and Cultures of Compliance, *Prometheus*, **34** (1), 49–62, doi:10.1080/08109028.2016.1222129.

McLysaght, E. (2011) Data Breach at Trinity College Dublin, *thejournal.ie*, 29 April.

McMenemy, D. (2017) *Privacy, Surveillance and the Information Profession: challenges, qualifications, and dilemmas?*, CILIP Privacy Briefing, CILIP.

Magi, T. J. (2010) A Content Analysis of Library Vendor Privacy Policies: do they meet our standards?, *College & Research Libraries*, May, 254–72.

Mai, J.-E. (2016) Big Data Privacy: the datafication of personal information, *Information Society*, **32** (3), 192–9, doi:10.1080/01972243.2016.1153010.

Marr, M. (2018) A Mother and Son Went to the Library: a drama played out in an unlikely place, cops say, *Miami Herald*, 13 August, www.miamiherald.com/news/state/florida/article216594625.html.

Marthews, A. and Tucker, C. (2015) *Government Surveillance and Internet Search Behavior*, MIT Sloan Working Paper no. 14380.

Masur, P. K., Teutsch, D. and Trepte, S. (2017) *Entwicklung und Validierung der Online-Privatheits-Kompetenzskala (OPLIS)* [Development and validation of the Online Privacy Literacy Scale (OPLIS)], Diagnostica, doi:10.1026/0012–1924/a000179.

Mathson, S. and Hancks, J. (2008) Privacy Please? A comparison between self-checkout and book checkout desk circulation rates for LGBT and other books, *Journal of Access Services*, **4** (3–4), 27–37.

Mayer-Schönberger, V. M. and Cukier, K. (2013) *Big Data: a revolution that will transform how we live, work, and think*, John Murray.

Miami-Dade Public Library System (2016) *Dear Patron*, press release, www.mdpls.org/news/press-releases/2016/overdrive.asp.

Miketa, A. (2012) *Library Diaries*, CreateSpace Independent Publishing Platform.

Miller, T. (2009) Social Security Numbers Found in Area Library Books, www.databreaches.net/oh-social-security-numbers-found-in-area-library-books.

Ministry of Justice (2015) *Revenge Porn: the facts: Be Aware B4 You Share*, https://assets.publishing.service.gov.uk/government/uploads/system/uploads/attachment_data/file/405286/revenge-porn-factsheet.pdf.

National Audit Office and Cabinet Office (2019) *Progress of the 2016–2021 National Cyber Security Programme: summary*.

National Cyber Security Centre (2016) *Ten Steps to Cyber-security*, www.ncsc.gov.uk/information/infographics-ncsc.

Nelson, F. (2014) Every 73 Seconds, Police Use Snooping Powers to Access Our Personal Records: who'll rein them in?, *The Spectator*, 11 October.

New Jersey State Library (2015) *The Librarian's Disaster Planning and Community Resiliency Guidebook: librarians fulfilling their role as information first responders*, www.njstatelib.org/wp-content/uploads/2015/09/The-Librarian-Guidebook-Sept-10-Final.pdf.

NISO (2015) NISO *Consensus Principles on Users' Digital Privacy in Library,*

Publisher, and Software-Provider Systems, https://groups.niso.org/apps/group_public/download.php/16064/NISO%20Privacy%20Principles.pdf.

Nissenbaum, H. (2010) *Privacy in Context: technology, policy, and the integrity of social life*, Stanford University Press.

Obar, J. A. and Oeldorf-Hirsch, A. (2016) *The Biggest Lie on the Internet: ignoring the privacy policies and terms of service policies of social networking services*, Working paper, York University, Michigan State University and University of Connecticut, http://ssrn.com/abstract=2757465.

O'Hara, K. and Stevens, D. (2006) *Inequality.com: Power, poverty and the digital divide*, OneWorld Publications.

Onwuemezi, N. (2018) Eighty Librarians Condemn Deal Between Home Office and SCL, *The Bookseller*, 5 June, www.thebookseller.com/news/library-workers-condemn-home-office-deal-797101.

Open University (2014) *Policy on Ethical Use of Student Data for Learning Analytics*.

Out-law.com (2014) BYOD Creates Potential Software Licensing Issue for Businesses, New Government Guidance Warns, *Out-law.com*, 7 October, www.out-law.com/en/articles/2014/october/byod-creates-potential-software-licensing-issue-for-businesses-new-government-guidance-warns.

Pariser, E. (2012) *The Filter Bubble: what the internet is hiding from you*, Penguin.

Parry, M. (2012) As Libraries Go Digital, Sharing of Data is at Odds With Tradition of Privacy, *Chronicle of Higher Education*, 5 November.

Pedersen, D. M. (1979) Dimensions of Privacy, *Perceptual and Motor Skills*, **48** (3 suppl), 1291–7.

Pedersen, D. M. (1997) Psychological Functions of Privacy, *Journal of Environmental Psychology*, **17** (2), 147–56.

Penney, J. (2016) Chilling Effects: online surveillance and Wikipedia use, *Berkeley Technology Law Journal*, **31** (1), 117–82.

Price, G. (2014) Hackers Breached Wyoming's Statewide Catalog 'WYLDCat' in Early October, *Library Journal*, 10 November, www.infodocket.com/2014/11/10/hackers-breached-wyomings-wyldcat-catalog-in-early-october.

Privacy Rights Clearinghouse (2012) www.privacyrights.org/data-breaches?title=library+systems+and+services.

Rainee, L. and Anderson, J. (2017) *Code-dependent: pros and cons of the algorithm age*, Pew Research Center.

Randall, D. P. and Newell, B. C. (2014) The Panoptic Librarian: the role of video surveillance in the modern public library, *iConference 2014 Proceedings*, 508–21, doi:10.9776/14132.

Reading Agency, Arts Council England, Society of Chief Librarians, National Association of Primary Care and Wellcome (2016) *Books on Prescription: how*

bibliotherapy can help your patients and save your practice time and money.
Richards, N. M. (2008) Intellectual Privacy, *Texas Law Review*, **87** (2), 387–445, http://ssrn.com/abstract=1108268.
Richards, N. M. (2011) The Limits of Tort Privacy, *Journal of Telecommunications and High Technology Law*, **9**, 357–84, http://ssrn.com/abstract=1862264.
Richards, N. M. (2015) *Intellectual Privacy: rethinking civil liberties in the digital age*, Oxford University Press.
Rubel, A. and Jones, K. (2014) *Student Privacy in Learning Analytics: an information ethics perspective*, Information Society, http://ssrn.com/abstract=2533704.
Rubel, A. and Zhang, M. (2015) Four Facets of Privacy and Intellectual Freedom in Licensing Contracts for Electronic Journals, *College & Research Libraries*, May, 427–49, doi:10.5860/crl.76.4.427.
Rubinstein, I. S. (2013) *Big Data: a pretty good privacy solution*, New York University School of Law.
Rubinstein, I. S. and Hartzog, W. (2016) Anonymization and Risk, *Washington Law Review*, **91**, 703–60.
Scottish PEN (2018) *Libraries for Privacy: a digital security and privacy toolkit.*
Shachaf, P. (2005) A Global Perspective On Library Association Codes Of Ethics, *Library & Information Science Research*, **27** (4), 513–33.
Sherriff, L. (2015) Staffordshire University Apologises for Accusing Student on Counter-terrorism Course of Terrorism, *Huffington Post*, 24 September.
Siegel, R. (2016) New Hampshire Library Defends use of Online Anonymity Software, *NPR.org*, 11 July.
Sieghart, W. (2014) *Independent Library Report for England*, Department for Culture, Media and Sport, www.gov.uk/government/publications/independent-library-report-for-england.
Solove, D. J. (2011) *Nothing to Hide: the false tradeoff between privacy and security*, Yale University Press.
Strachan, G. (2016) Cop Counters Move into Angus Libraries as Part of One-stop Shop Programme, *The Courier*, 22 August.
Sturges, P., Iliffe, U. and Dearnley, J. (2001) *Privacy in the Digital Library Environment.*
Swartz, N. (2004) Offshoring Privacy, *Information Management Journal*, September/October, 24–6.
Timmons, H. (2015) Security Breach at LexisNexis Now Appears Larger, *New York Times*, 13 April, www.nytimes.com/2005/04/13/technology/security-breach-at-lexisnexis-now-appears-larger.html.
Tockar, A. (2014) Riding with the Stars: passenger privacy in the NYC taxicab

dataset, *Neustar*, 15 September, https://research.neustar.biz/2014/09/15/ridingwiththestarspassengerprivacyinthenyctaxicabdataset.

Travis, S. (2010) Library Service Software Glitch Creates Student Data Breach at 6 Fla. Colleges, *Sun Sentinel*, 11 August, https://phys.org/pdf200719381.pdf.

Tummon, N. and McKinnon, D. (2018) Attitudes and Practices of Canadian Academic Librarians Regarding Library and Online Privacy: a national study, *Library & Information Science Research*, **40** (2), 86–97, doi:https://doi.org/10.1016/j.lisr.2018.05.002.

Vermillion, J. K. (2009) Why We're Not Digitizing Zines, *Duke University library blog*, 21 September, https://blogs.library.duke.edu/digital-collections/2009/09/21/why-were-not-digitizing-zines.

Warren, M. (2016) Toronto Public Library Reveals its Website Searches in Real Time, *Metro Toronto*, 21 July.

Warren, S. and Brandeis, L. (1890) The Right to Privacy, *Harvard Law Review*, **IV** (5).

Weale, S. (2017) London University Tells Students Their E-Mails May Be Monitored, *The Guardian*, 20 January.

Webster, P. (2003) Intrepid Library Thief Brought to Book, *The Age*, 20 June, www.theage.com.au/articles/2003/06/19/1055828433775.html.

West, J. (2016) Cybersecurity as an Extension of Privacy in Libraries, *Computers in Libraries*, June, 24–5.

Westin, A. F. (1967) *Privacy and Freedom*, Atheneum.

Wharton, L. (2018) Ethical Implications of Digital Tools and Emerging Roles for Academic Librarians. In Fernandez, P. D. and Tilton, K. (eds), *Applying Library Values to Emerging Technology: decision-making in the age of open access, maker spaces, and the ever-changing library*, Publications in Librarianship 72, American Library Association, 35–54.

Wiegand, W. (2002) This Month, 85 Years Ago, *American Libraries*, **33** (10), 74.

Wilber, D. Q. (2008) Pair Charged in Identity Theft Scheme, *Washington Post*, 11 December.

Wise, P. (2015) Library Privacy Policies in 2015: strategies for renewed relevance, *CUNY Academic Works*, 8 May.

Witherden, G. (2017) Library Volunteer Raises Privacy Concerns Over New Customer Service Hubs, *Maidenhead Advertiser*, 18 August, www.maidenhead-advertiser.co.uk/gallery/maidenhead/119865/library-volunteer-raises-privacy-concerns-over-new-customer-service-hubs.html.

Wohlgemuth, S., Sonehara, N. and Muller, G. (2010) *Tagging Disclosures of Personal Data to Third Parties to Preserve Privacy*, Springer.

Women's Institute (2013) *On Permanent Loan? Community managed libraries: the volunteer perspective.*

Woodward, J. (2007) *What Every Librarian Should Know About Electronic Privacy*, Libraries Unlimited.

Wylie, A. (2014) Volunteers and Data Protection, *Voices for the Library*, 28 January.

Zimmer, M. (2015) Privacy and Cloud Computing in Public Libraries: the case of BiblioCommons, *iConference 2015*.

Zine Libraries (2015) *Zine Librarians Code of Ethics Zine*, http://zinelibraries.info/code-of-ethics.

Zuboff, S. (2019) *The Age of Surveillance Capitalism: the fight for the future at the new frontier of power*, Profile Books.

Glossary of terms

Chilling effect The effect whereby users either know or suspect that they are being monitored, and change their behaviour accordingly.

Co-location is the practice of placing several services in a single location.

Cryptoparty is a public workshop or event at which attendees have an opportunity to learn about cryptography, such as virtual private networks, encryption or the Tor anonymity network.

Data breach *see* Personal data breach.

Data controller means the natural or legal person, public authority, agency or other body which, alone or jointly with others, determines the purposes and means of the processing of personal data.

Data processor means a natural or legal person, public authority, agency or other body which processes personal data on behalf of the data controller.

Data shadows are the data generated about individuals by others.

Datafication is the term used by Mai (2016) to consider a new model (the datafication model) wherein new personal information is deduced by employing predictive analytics on already gathered data.

Digital footprint refers to the data you leave behind when you go online. It's what you've said, what others have said about you, where you've been, images you're tagged in, personal information, social media profiles and much more.

Dooced refers to getting fired for something you wrote on your blog or on social media.

Filter bubble is a term used by Pariser (2012) to describe a state of intellectual isolation resulting from the use of data about an individual - such as their previous search history - being used by algorithms to selectively guess what information a user would like to see.

Learner analytics is the measurement, collection, analysis and reporting of data about learners and the use of this data to improve learning and teaching.

Mosaic effect refers to the features within a dataset that, in combination with other data, identifies individuals.

Packet sniffing is the act of capturing packets of data flowing across a computer network.

Personal data breach refers to 'a breach of security leading to the accidental or unlawful destruction, loss, alteration, unauthorised disclosure of, or access to, personal data transmitted, stored or otherwise processed' (Article 4 (12) of the GDPR).

Refgrunt is here used to refer to librarian bloggers venting publicly on their blogs about their interactions with patrons.

Revenge porn is 'The sharing of private, sexual materials, either photos or videos, of another person without their consent and with the purpose of causing embarrassment or distress. The images are sometimes accompanied by personal information about the subject, including their full name, address and links to their social media profiles' (Ministry of Justice, 2015).

Session hijacking is the exploitation of a valid computer session in order to gain unauthorized access to information or services in a computer system.

Streisand effect is the phenomenon whereby the very act of trying to ensure that information remains private has the opposite effect.

Surveillance capitalism is 'A new economic order that claims human experience as raw material for hidden commercial practices of extraction, prediction and sales' (Zuboff, 2019).

Upskirting is the act of covertly photographing underneath someone's clothing without their consent.

Warrant canary is a statement saying that an institution has not received secret requests for user data by government or law enforcement officers.

Index